Soul Sculpture

SOUL SCULPTURE

Compiled by
E. F. & L. Harvey

British Address
Harvey Christian Publishers UK
PO Box 510, Cheadle
Stoke-on-Trent, ST10 2NQ
Tel/Fax (01538) 752291
E-mail: jjcook@mac.com

United States Address
Harvey Christian Publishers Inc.
3107 Hwy. 321
Hampton, TN 37658
Tel/Fax (423) 768-2297
E-mail: books@harveycp.com
Website: www.harveycp.com

Copyright © 1957

First Edition 1957
Ninth Edition 2006

Printed in USA

All rights reserved. No part of this book may be reproduced or transmitted in any form or by any means, electronic or mechanical, including photocopying, recording, or by any information storage and retrieval system without written permission from the publisher, except for the inclusion of brief quotations in a review.

Cover design by Scott Yule

ISBN-13: 978-1-932774-02-3
ISBN-10: 1-932774-02-5

Printed by
Old Paths Tract Society Inc.
Shoals, Indiana 47581

ACKNOWLEDGMENTS

We have deeply appreciated the courteous replies which have been received from both authors and publishers in asking permission to use copyright material for this book. We would take this opportunity to express our thanks for the kindness afforded in the following instances:

A. & C. Black, Ltd., for the poem by Ella Wheeler Wilcox; Oswald Chambers Publications for the extract from the writings of Oswald Chambers; The China Inland Mission for the quotations by Dr. and Mrs. Howard Taylor; Peter Davies, Ltd., for the extract by Peter Marshall; The Reader's Digest Association, Ltd., for the passage by Philip Wylie; The Dohnavur Fellowship for the poem by Amy Carmichael; The Evangelical Publishers for the poems by Nell Ruth Roffe, Meredith Gray, Grace Noll Crowell, and Fanny Allen, and the quotation by J. H. Hunter; the Editor of *The Flame* for the poem, "Mother's Question"; Prebendary J. E. S. Harrison for his poem; Miss Fay Inchfawn for her poems; Dr. Bob Jones for the poem, "The Teacher's Crown"; the college periodical, *Fellowship News*, for the story of Billy Sunday; the Editor of *Joyful News* for the poems by Mrs. Clara Simpson; The Reilly & Lee Company for the two poems by Edgar A. Guest; Lillenas Publishing Co. for the two song poems, "Father of Mine" and "God Give Us Homes"; the Editor of *Moody Monthly* for the poems by Frances R. Longing, Gertrude Ryder Bennett, and David F. Nygren; Mrs. Kathryn Blackburn Peck for her poem, "Mothers the World Needs"; Stirling Tract Enterprise for the poems by Eva I. Travers; the Editor of *The Wesleyan Methodist* for the poems, "Wanted: A Man" and "The Planter" by Wilma Burton; Marshall, Morgan & Scott, Ltd., for the quotations by S. D. Gordon.

As quotations and poems have been gleaned from many sources, it has not been possible, in every case, to trace the author. As Christian publishers we trust that such persons will understand that it has not been our intention to violate literary courtesies.

CONTENTS

I	The Task—Soul Sculpture	11
II	The Gift Entrusted	17
III	The Vision	25
IV	The Preparation of the Sculptress	33
V	Mother—Soul Sculptress	41
VI	Father as Sculptor	57
VII	Home—The Workshop	69
VIII	Full-Time or Part-Time Sculptors?	79
IX	The Family Studies the Master Sculptor's Plans	87
X	The Chiseling	99
XI	Other Sculptors	111
XII	Chips from the Chisel	119

FOREWORD

Various influences have moved us to make this effort. The response to a "Home Page" often run in *The Message of Victory*, has shown the felt need for such material. Inquiries made through bookshops and the mail have convinced us that many parents, educators, and youth workers of today are reaching out for that which will help and inspire them as they labor at the task of child-rearing, made so very difficult by the trend of the age.

In our evangelistic travels in the interests of revival, a conviction has grown that revival in the home is a first essential. Christ must be brought back into the home as "Head of the House," if revival is to visit this land.

It is not the purpose of this work to instruct as to methods of teaching, discipline, etc. It is our purpose to leave the reader with a sense of responsibility, with a vision of possibility, and with a promise of success through God. In order to give the book cohesion, we have had to introduce some thoughts of our own. However, we have been as sparing with these as was possible considering the great variety of extracts and authors introduced.

The last chapter of the book contains a miscellany of quotations, which, we trust, will prove an added resource for pastors and Sunday School teachers.

Guidance has been sought, and much prayer has gone into this volume. We send it forth confident that He Who said, "Suffer the little children to come unto me," will bless it to many in the interests of that rising generation so desperately in need of help and guidance.

Edwin and Lillian Harvey
August 14th, 1957.

PUBLISHERS' FOREWORD

Soul Sculpture was first published in 1957 in the UK and, having been reproduced from the original many times, we thought it time to reset the book completely. Thanks to the voluntary labors of some good friends in Wisconsin to whom we are very grateful, the book was put on disc and then finally edited by us.

As punctuation rules have changed over the years, we have updated the text accordingly. We have also had, occasionally, to change the position of a poem in order to conserve space, and in at least one instance, added a poem or two to fill up an extra page. In several places, the authors have used references which date the book; we have left these untouched.

In our more recent books, we have taken pains to cite the page and book from which each quotation has been taken. In the first edition of *Soul Sculpture* this was not done, but an acknowledgment page was inserted instead where the authors expressed their thanks to certain publishers for quotations taken from their books, but further details were not mentioned. As it would be virtually impossible to trace the source of every quote used, we have retained the original acknowledgment page and trust that any oversight on our part will be pardoned.

We now publish this new edition of *Soul Sculpture* with thankfulness for the blessing it has been to many families over the past years, and with the prayer that it may continue to encourage all those concerned with the upbringing of children; may they realize what a stupendous privilege it is to be chosen by God to be a "soul sculpture."

Barry & Trudy Tait.
Harvey Christian Publishers
June, 2003.

THE SCULPTURE

I am a sculptor. I work in the dark.
    If my hand slip,
I mar for a lifetime perhaps—dull the Spark,
    Or seal the lip.

My tools are so fine that they may not be seen—
    Yet mould and shape
Flesh, bone, nerve, and brain to forms noble or mean—
    Angel or Ape.

O, steady my hand, Thou that gavest the Clay;
    Make clear my sight!
With all of me, Lord, I entreat and I pray
    That I chisel right.

—Flores Folsom.

CHAPTER 1

THE TASK—SOUL SCULPTURE

No hearts but those of parents can know the strange conflict of emotions—joy and awe—as they take into their arms for the first time that little bundle of life. As they gaze into the eyes of their babe, they must, if at all serious-minded, feel a sense of grave responsibility in that they have been entrusted with the greatest of tasks. Jointly they are to shape this immortal soul into a thing of beauty or baseness—into a force for good or evil—towards a destiny in Heaven or in hell. Every act of their lives, from this moment, is a chiseling influence upon that piece of living marble. They are the sculptors of a soul.

The thought is by no means a new one, but many authors, both in poetry and prose, have used various pictures to convey the same sentiment. In the following poem, Bessie Chandler uses the metaphor of pruning to illustrate the sculpturing of a soul:

SOUL-GARDENING

"O, my child, my pure and perfect man-child,
    With the light of Heaven in your eyes,
And your yellow hair like glory resting
    O'er a face so angel-sweet and wise!

"O, my child, I hold your hand and tremble
    When I think of all that you must meet
On the way, where there is naught to guide you
    Save my clouded eyes and stumbling feet.

"Is the gardener not appalled and daunted
    When he sees but leafless twigs, and knows
That within the bare, brown thing there slumbers
    Waiting for his waking hand, the rose?

"So I fear from fingers all unskillful
   Some rude touch your perfect growth may mar;
If the pruning knife slips but a little,
   You must carry all your life the scar.

"O, my child, unknown, unconscious currents
   Meet and mingle in your young, warm blood!
So, God help me, when your soul shall blossom,
   And—God help me should I blight its bud."

A still different metaphor is used by the well-known writer, J. H. Hunter, to express the same thought:

"The other day I saw a barricade erected on the sidewalk around a newly-laid piece of cement that it might have time to dry and harden before being used by pedestrians. But someone had inadvertently 'put his foot in it.'

"We have all seen these clearly defined footprints in the sidewalk, made when the cement was soft, and hardened at last into an indelible print to remain for all time. It was not a mark placed there maliciously, but simply a blundering foot of someone so intent on his own business that he did not heed anything else beside, but left a mark that remains. The hard surface tells nothing more of his coming and his going save that one, marring print that will endure as long as the sidewalk itself.

"There are many souls in the world that bear the marks of blundering feet. These may have been made when the world for them was young, but now that it has grown old and they with it, they still carry the scar or scars of the blundering feet.

"How easy it is to leave a mark on a young life by a blundering foot. It is not a deliberate wound that is inflicted. Just some slighting remark, some repression of a youthful idea or ideal, the faith or exuberance of youth made light of, a generous love thwarted by someone intent on airing his own views and too ignorant of the sensitive, plastic nature with which he deals to know that he is leaving a lifelong scar. Ridicule, an example of irreverence, a coarse jest, may leave a disfiguring mark on some soul that time will never efface."

Sad to say, some parents do fail in their God-entrusted task, as is expressed in the following poem by Gertrude Ryder Bennett:

AS THE TWIG

"We, the youth who shock you so,
Ask, 'How much did you help us grow?'
You gaze at us with astonishment.
Where were you when the twig was bent?
If you wanted saplings tall and straight,
Why did you wait? Why did you wait?
You gave us bread. Did that atone
For the days and nights we were left alone?
You laughed our heroes from their height
And left them worthless in our sight.
They lost their standards in the dust;
Their weapons dulled with bitter rust.
And when we asked for God, you turned
Our answers back with doubt that burned.
We watched you tempt the hand of fate.
The world plunged into war and hate
In mockery of brother-love;
Nothing on earth, nothing above!
You blame us for skirting danger's brink—
We want to feel, for we dare not think.
Who asks good fruit from a well-grown tree
Must take the time for husbandry."

While walking around a garden one day, a child was asked why he thought a certain tree grew crooked. "S'pose somebody must have stepped on it when it was a little fellow," was the thoughtful reply.

We pass from this sobering thought of the danger of marring that precious thing in our hands to that of the inspiring task that is ours. We may know that He Who has entrusted into our hands the noblest and most enduring of all labors, will grant the vision to plan and the skill to shape.

To every mother comes the call to be
An adept in life's finest artistry—
To mould a plastic to a great design
That will remain forever strong and fine.
The work God gives to motherhood alone
Is like in beauty to His very own,
Which is to bring forth life and make it whole
By weaving all Himself into each soul.
—Unknown.

What if God should place in your hand a diamond, and tell you to inscribe on it a sentence which should be read at the last day, and be shown then as an index of your own thoughts and feelings? What care, what caution, would you exercise in the selection? Now, this is what God has done. He has placed before you the immortal minds of your children, more imperishable than the diamond on which you are about to inscribe every day and every hour, by your instructions, by your spirit, or by your example, something which will remain and be exhibited for or against you at the judgment day.
—Dr. Payson.

THE PLANTER

One man ploughed an open field
    And planted winter wheat;
His labor lasted a year — until
    The harvest was replete.

Another wanted his work to endure
    His lifetime through, and so
He planted a tree of oak, and then
    With pride he watched it grow.

Another planned for eternity,
    And with diligence and manner mild,
He planted a true and noble thought
    In the heart of a little child.
—Wilma Burton.

If you write upon a paper, a careless hand may destroy it.

If you write upon parchment, the dust of centuries may gather over it.

If you write upon marble, the moss may cover it and the elements may erase it.

If you engrave your thoughts with a pen of iron upon the granite cliff, in the slow revolving years it shall wear away, and when the earth melts your writings will perish.

Write them on the heart of a child. There engrave your thoughts and they shall endure, when the world shall pass away, and the stars shall fall, and time shall be no more. For that heart is immortal, and your words written there shall live all through eternity.—Anon.

BUILDING TEMPLES

A builder builded a temple;
    He wrought with grace and skill—
Pillars and groins and arches
    All fashioned to work his will.
Men said, as they saw its beauty,
    "It shall never know decay.
Great is thy skill, O builder;
    Thy fame shall endure for aye."

A teacher builded a temple
    With loving and infinite care,
Planning each arch with patience,
    Laying each stone with prayer.
None praised his unceasing efforts,
    None knew of his wondrous plan;
For the temple the teacher builded
    Was unseen by the eyes of man.

Gone is the builder's temple,
    Crumbled into the dust;
Low lies each stately pillar,
    Food for consuming rust.
But the temple the teacher builded
    Will last while the ages roll;
For that beautiful, unseen temple
    Is a child's immortal soul.

            —Unknown.

A sweet, new blossom of Humanity,
Fresh fallen from God's own home to flower on earth.
—George Massey.

As living jewels dropped unstained from Heaven.
—Pollock.

A lovely being, scarcely formed or molded;
A rose with all its sweetest leaves yet folded.
—Lord Byron.

CHAPTER II

THE GIFT ENTRUSTED

It has taken poet minds to beautifully express the gift of a new life. That a child is a gift straight from Heaven is a fact that has been accepted by nobler minds from the beginning of time. The Bible abounds with sentiments recognizing this beautiful truth.

"Who are those with thee?" asked a brother of the old Patriarch Jacob as he looked upon his eleven children. "The children which God hath graciously given thy servant," was the answer. And later Jacob, now a grandfather, asked the same question of his son Joseph, and received a similar answer, "They are my sons, whom God hath given me."

The Psalmist utters the same sentiment, "Children are an heritage of the Lord." In the oldest book of the Bible we have a grand expression of the identical thought, "The Spirit of God hath made me, and the breath of the Almighty hath given me life" (Job 33:4).

—E. & L. Harvey.

> If there is anything that will endure
> The eye of God, because it still is pure,
> It is the spirit of a little child,
> Fresh from His hand, and therefore undefiled.
> —R. H. Stoddard.

The newborn babe is a fresh act of God. He is the latest revelation of God's creative handiwork. He is God's last messenger to earth . . . The babe face is a new window of Heaven. Through it the upper-world folks look down upon us. And through it we look up to them, gathered about the Father in the upper Home. In those babe eyes the Father Himself is looking into our eyes, and we may look up into His. Each babe is a fresh touch of Eden's purity and beauty. He tells us of the early Eden life long ago, and of the new Eden life—far ahead—maybe less far than we think.

—S. D. Gordon.

> They are idols of hearts and of households;
>   They are angels of God in disguise;
> His sunlight still sleeps in their tresses,
>   His glory still gleams in their eyes;
> Those truants from home and from Heaven,
>   They have made me more manly and mild;
> And I know now how Jesus could liken
>   The kingdom of God to a child.
>   —Charles M. Dickenson.

A little child, according to the canons of the market, is just about the most worthless thing going. He cannot sow, or reap, or spin. He does not understand even the benefits that are bestowed upon him. A child stands as near to the seed-form as he can; he is only an acorn. No matter whether he grows to be an oak or not, he is nothing but a seed, an acorn. He is the lowest in society. "And yet," says the Savior, "this lowest thing in human life, a little child, is so sacred before God, that whosoever accepts him in the fullness of the recognition that he is God's child, shall be counted to have received God Himself; and whoever despises him, or causes him in any way to stumble, had better never been born."

Such is the teaching of Christ as to the value of human nature —not as to the value of fully developed and educated human nature, that stands in the economies of human life in all its usefulness—but take the lowest form of it, its zero, and yet, intrinsically, it has such a value that on no other occasion and in regard to no other person were there such words uttered as by the Lord Jesus in regard to a little child.—H. W. Beecher.

The Beautiful Presence hides itself more in babes than men. It is marvelous in our eyes, that where there is neither physical might, nor rational might, *there* the God of all might should be so much the more. . . . "Out of the mouths of babes and sucklings hast Thou ordained strength because of Thine enemies, that Thou mightest still the enemy and the avenger."—John Pulsford in *Quiet Thoughts*.

THE BABY

Another little wave
    Upon the sea of life;
Another soul to save,
    Amid the toil and strife.
Two more little feet
    To walk the dusty road;
To choose where two paths meet,
    The narrow and the broad.

Two more little hands,
    To work for good or ill;
Two more little eyes;
    Another little will;
Another heart to love,
    Receiving love again;
And so the baby came,
    A thing of joy and pain.
        —*Providence Journal.*

The birth of a babe is a mighty event. From the frequency of births, as well as the frequency of deaths, we are prone to set a very low estimate on the ushering into existence of an animate child, unless the child be born in a palace or some other lofty station. Unless there be something extraordinary in the circumstances, we do not attach the importance we ought to the event itself. It is only noble birth, distinguished birth, that is chronicled in the journals or announced with salvos of artillery. I admit that the relations of a prince, of a president and statesman are more important to their fellow-men and touch them at more points than those of an obscure pauper, but when the events are weighed in the scales of eternity, the difference is scarcely perceptible.

    In the darkest hovel in Brooklyn, in the dingiest attic or cellar, or in any place in which a human being sees the first glimpse of light, the eye of the Omniscient beholds an occurrence of prodigious moment. A life is begun, a life that shall never end. A heart begins to throb that shall beat to the keenest delight or the acutest anguish. More than this—a soul commences a career that shall outlast the earth on which it moves. The soul enters upon an existence that shall be untouched by time, when the sun is extinguished like a taper in the sky, the moon blotted out, and the heavens have been rolled together as a vesture and changed forever.—Theodore Cuyler.

> O child! O newborn denizen
> Of life's great city! On thy head
> The glory of the morn is shed,
> Like a celestial benison!
> Here at the portal thou dost stand,
> And with thy little hand
> Thou openest thy mysterious gate
> Into the future's undiscovered land.
> —Longfellow.

"Life is God's gift: your trust and mine. We are the trustees of the Giver." Although the little life is a gift to us, the length of that life is determined by God alone, and therefore we need to view it as a loan.

TO ALL PARENTS

"I'll lend you for a little time a child of Mine," He said,
"For you to love the while she lives and mourn for when she's dead.
It may be six or seven years, or twenty-two or three,
But will you, till I call her back, take care of her for Me?
She'll bring her charms to gladden you, and should her stay be brief,
You'll have her lovely memories as solace for your grief.

"I cannot promise she will stay, since all from earth return.
But there are lessons taught down there I want this child to learn.
I've looked the wide world over in My search for teachers true,
And from the throngs that crowd life's lanes I have selected you.
Now will you give her all your love, nor think the labor vain,
Nor hate Me when I come to call to take her back again?"

I fancied that I heard them say, "Dear Lord, Thy will be done!
For all the joy Thy child shall bring, the risk of grief we'll run.
We'll shelter her with tenderness, we'll love her while we may,
And for the happiness we've known, forever grateful stay;
But should the angels call for her much sooner than we've planned,
We'll brave the bitter grief that comes and try to understand.

("To All Parents" is from the book, *All In A Lifetime* by Edgar A. Guest. Copyright 1938, The Reilly & Lee Co., Chicago, IL., U.S.A.)

Catherine Booth, the mother of seven children, gives this advice: "One of the most important questions for a parent to answer is: 'To whom does this child belong? Is it mine, or is it the Lord's?'" Many a Christian parent has dedicated the new life to God and His service, and a peculiar blessing has rested upon those children so dedicated.

"And they brought unto him also infants, that he would touch them" (Luke 18:15).

Hannah, of Bible fame, gave a son to judge Israel in a time of deep national need. Do we not admire the wisdom of God in taking a weak little boy, dedicated by a praying mother to God's service, and setting him down in the temple as a contrast and rebuke to an indulgent, careless father and two wicked sons? The secret of what made Samuel so special can be found in the words of Hannah before her son's birth: "If thou wilt give unto thine handmaid a man child, then will I give him unto the Lord all the days of his life" (I Sam. 1:11). And the vows were paid as is shown by her words later: "For this child I prayed; and the Lord hath given me my petition which I asked of him: therefore also I have lent him to the Lord: as long as he liveth he shall be lent to the Lord" (I Sam. 1:27, 28). How God honored this mother's utter dedication may be seen in the following few but meaningful words: "And the child Samuel grew before the Lord" (I Sam. 2:21). "And Samuel grew, and the Lord was with him" (I Sam. 3:19).

Grattan Guinness, the writer and evangelist, teacher and father, wrote thus when a little daughter came into their home:

> "One cloud remains, that by thy birth
> Thou enterest a ruined earth,
>   My little One.
>
> "But thou shalt find with sweet surprise,
> Earth but a pathway to the skies,
>   My little One.
>
> "Such is our trust, for Lord, we give
> Thy gift to Thee! O then receive
>   Our little One.
>
> "Receive her Lord, and let her be
> Thine own to all eternity—
>   Thy little One."

God again honored this dedication by developing and blessing the gifts and powers of Geraldine Guinness, later to become Mrs. Howard Taylor. For many years her biographies have blessed thousands of readers. Her niece, in writing her aunt's life story, has called her book, "Her Web of Time," an expressive reminder that, right from the beginning, Geraldine's life had been a brief loan from the Lord, to Whom she belonged to all eternity!—E. & L. Harvey.

What a significant thing it is when we dedicate a little child to God! Do we stop to recall, in such a moment, that in a million years that soul will be living and mounting higher and higher, or dropping lower and lower? And the solemn thing about it all is that it will bear the impress which we place upon it. This makes the position of a parent or teacher unutterably solemn and emphasizes the tremendous importance of Sunday Schools.—Unknown.

With such a task before us, we might well pray:

> "God! Who gavest into my guiding hand this wanderer,
> To lead her through a world whose darkling paths
> I tread with steps so faltering—leave not me
> To bring her to the gates of Heaven, alone!
> I feel my feebleness. Let these stay on—
> The angels who now visit her in dreams!
> Bid them be near her pillow till in death
> The closed eyes look upon Thy face once more,
> And let the light and music, which the world
> Borrows of Heaven, and which her infant sense
> Hails with sweet recognition, be to her
> A voice to call her upward, and a lamp
> To lead her steps unto Thee!"

MY WISH FOR MY BABE

Son, the sight of your downy wee head fills my heart with many longings—desires strong and tender, dreams bright and rosy, hopes high and worthy, ambitions great and lofty, and all for you!

Down the years I see a path stretching away and away and away. You have already begun your journey upon that long road. I can be with you only a little while, and then you must travel on alone. But "there is a Guide Who never falters, and while He leads, you cannot stray." He stands aside now at the opening of the way, waiting to go with you, to the close. So my first and greatest wish for you, my son, is that you early reach up, putting your little hand in His, and "let Jesus lead, He knows the way." He will guide you into all truth, so that you will be led unto manly boyhood and noble manhood.

I shall not attempt to choose your profession for you. I want it to be God's choice, not mine. To glorify Him is life's highest attainment, so to be in His appointed place and will is my loftiest desire for your life.—Unknown.

THREE MASONS

Once a man came upon three rock masons at work. "What are you doing?" he asked of them.

"I'm carving these stones into the different sizes wanted," answered the first.

"I'm earning six dollars a day," replied the second.

"I'm helping to build a great cathedral," commented the last.

Only he had caught the vision of the great work that he was helping to do.

THREE MOTHERS

Once a woman came upon three mothers at work. "What are you doing?" she asked of them.

"I'm doing the weekly washing," answered the first.

"I'm doing a bit of household drudgery," replied the second.

"I'm mothering three young children who some day will fill important and useful spheres in life, and wash-day is a part of my grand task in caring for these souls who shall live forever," replied the third. Only she had caught the vision of the great work she was doing.

—Anon.

CHAPTER III

THE VISION

It takes vision to give the proper incentive for the successful completion of any task. The farmer who visualizes the harvested grain, thinks nothing of rising early and working late. The student who foresees a successful practice, is willing to forego lovely home comforts and associations and live in a garret in a strange city. The artist who has, in his imagination, painted the finished masterpiece, will work arduously, not counting the thousands of brushstrokes which to others would appear meaningless daubs.

The Good Book says, "Where there is no vision, the people perish" (Prov. 29:18). In no sphere is this more true than in that of parenthood. The parent who has impressed upon his soul the vision of the finished creation of the little ones entrusted to his care, will not begrudge the seeming waste of many years of loving toil. A famous mother whose seven children grew to be philanthropists, preachers, composers, writers, reformers and missionaries, early caught such a vision. Each night when tucking them in, the mother whispered, "The world is waiting for you." Such constant chiseling could not fail to fulfil the angelic vision.

Many a thoughtless, flippant remark has deeply wounded the parents of large families. "Rearing a brood of little brats," is all some ignorant, vision-blind humans can see. It reminds us of the story of the world-famous sculptor, Story, who was a lawyer in his early years:

"One day the smoldering fires of an artist's instinct burst forth within him, and he threw up his lucrative practice and went to Rome at the behest of his 'Voices.' A materially-minded American friend years later watched him at work in his studio. To see this once promising member of the Bar working with clay was too much for the visitor: 'Story, what under the heavens made you give up your splendid practice in America and come out here to pinch mud?'"

Parents would do well to ignore, as Story did, the thoughtless chatter of souls who live with no vision.—E. & L. Harvey.

> Untried material;
>   Clay yet unwrought;
> Future, ethereal;
>   Powers unthought;
> No angel can measure
>   The breadth of your span,
> Nor mete out for treasure
>   The reach of a man.
>   —Fay Inchfawn.

And the babe is yet more a marvel of possibility. The man who will sway thousands to his will as the whirlwind sweeps the forest, lies sleeping in that babe. The organizer of the world's industries, or the leader of the world's thought, or the changer of the world's life and of the map of the earth, is in that wee morsel of humanity lying in his mother's arms.

That cooing voice may compel the whole world to listen. Those fat, dainty fingers may pen words that a world will be eager to read. A Wesley or a Faraday may be there, only waiting the coming of his day of action. And, far more than these, the man who will re-live Jesus' life, with all its simplicity and purity and fragrance, in some humble corner, that will touch and tinge deeply the life of the crowd, may lie there all open to the impress of father and mother.

—S. D. Gordon.

I'D RATHER

> I'd rather be a mother
>   Than anyone on earth,
> Bringing up a child or two
>   Of unpretentious birth.
>
> I'd rather tuck a little child
>   All safe and sound in bed—
> Than twine a chain of diamonds
>   About my foolish head.

> I'd rather wash a smudgy face
>   With round, bright baby eyes—
> Than paint the pageantry of fame,
>   Or walk among the wise.
>   —Meredith Gray.

Yesterday I rode past a field where a boy was plowing. The lad's hair stuck out through the top of his hat; he was bony and awkward; one suspender held his trousers in place; his bare legs and arms were brown and sunburned and briar-scarred.

He swung his horses around as I passed, and from under the flapping brim of his hat he cast a quick glance out of dark, half-bashful eyes and modestly returned my salute.

Who knows, I may go to that boy to borrow money, or to hear him preach, or to beg him to defend me in a lawsuit; or he may stand with pulse unhastened, bare of arm, in white apron, ready to do his duty, while the cone is placed over my face, and night and death come creeping into my veins.

Be patient with boys—you are dealing with soul-stuff. Destiny waits just around the comer. Be patient with boys. —Elbert Hubbard.

A SNUB-NOSED BOY

"He's only a snub-nosed small boy," you say.
  Speak kindly to him when you can,
Because the snub-nosed, small boy of today
  Will become tomorrow—a man.

"What kind of a man will he be?" you ask.
  As the tree is bent, so 'twill grow;
For every success there was first a task,
  It will ever be true, you know.

'Tis easier to train the young boy aright,
  Than to wait till a later day;
Pointing him daily to Jesus, the Light;
  Than to wait till he's gone astray.

> He's only a snub-nosed, small boy today,
> With sparkling eyes and cheeks of tan;
> But start him aright, if ever you may,
> For tomorrow, he is a man.
> —J. A. Rowell.

DESCRIPTION OF A BOY

After a male baby has grown out of long clothes and triangles and has acquired pants, freckles and so much dirt that relatives do not care to kiss it between meals, it becomes a BOY.

A boy is nature's answer to that false belief that there is no such thing as perpetual motion. A boy can swim like a fish, run like a deer, climb like a squirrel, bellow like a bull, eat like a pig, or act like a mule according to climatic conditions. He is a piece of skin stretched over an appetite; a noise covered with smudges. He is called a tornado because he comes at the most unexpected times and leaves everything a wreck behind him.

He is a growing child of superlative promise, to be fed, watered, and kept warm; a joy, a periodic nuisance, the problem of our times, the hope of a nation. HIS FUTURE IS IN OUR HANDS, GOD BLESS HIM.

WHAT IS A BOY?

He is a person who will carry on what you have started.

He is to sit right where you are sitting, and attend, when you are gone, to those things you think are so important.

You may adopt all the policies you please, but how they will be carried out depends upon him.

Even if you make leagues and treaties, he will have to manage them.

He will sit at your place in the House of Commons, and occupy your position on the Supreme Bench.

He will assume control of your cities and nation.

He will move in and take over your prisons, churches, schools, universities, and corporations.

All your work will be judged and praised or condemned by him. Your reputation and your future are in his hands.

All your work is for him, and the fate of the nation and of humanity is in his hands.

So it might be well to pay him some attention.—*Wise Counsel.*

The mother of Robert Fulton, the inventor of the steamboat, early visualized what her boy's possibilities were. "I grew up under the care of my blessed mother," says Robert. "She developed my early talent for drawing, and encouraged me in my visits to the machine-shops of the town."

Because Robert was a poor pupil at school, his teacher complained to the mother, who gave this far-sighted answer: "My boy's head, sir, is so full of original notions that there is no vacant chamber in which to store the contents of your musty books."

"I was only ten years old at that time," said Fulton. "My mother seemed to be the only human being who understood my natural bent for mechanics."

Thomas Edison, another inventor whose discoveries have contributed much to the efficiency of our times, likewise had a mother with a vision. After he had been at school for three months, his teacher sent him home, claiming he was too stupid to learn. His mother took over the task of teaching her son, and later in life he declared that his mother's faith in him and her patience in helping him to learn, were largely responsible for his achievements.

In a classroom in Germany many years ago, an unusual teacher named Trebonius always doffed his hat when he entered the schoolroom. "For," he explained, "some of my scholars may become burgomasters, generals, authors, and cardinals in future days." The vision of such a man was well justified by the history of at least one of those boys who became none other than the great reformer, Martin Luther. —E. & L. Harvey.

I was in the company of a talented Christian lady when a friend said to her, "Why have you never written a book?"

"I am writing two," was the quiet reply. "Have been engaged on one for ten years, the other five."

"You surprise me," cried the friend. "What profound works they must be!"

"It doth not appear yet what we shall be," was her reply, "but when He makes up His jewels, my great ambition is to find them there."

"Your children?" I asked.

"Yes, my two children. They are my life work."—*Christian Age.*

It is said of an old Roman general that when he heard the old men shout, on a great procession-day, "We have been brave!" that he sighed and said, "When they can no longer go to battle, who will take care of the country?" And when the young men came, in all the flush of their noble manhood and said, "We are brave!" the old man sighed and said, "Alas! these, too, will soon be gone, and who will take care of the country then?"

After a while it was said, "Here come the children." Then the old man leaned upon his staff and listened to catch their shout; and at last he caught it, as it was wafted on the breeze, and as their clear, loud voices rang out, this was their cry, "We will be brave!" And the old man's heart leaped up within him, and the fire flashed from his eyes as he said, "It is enough; the country is safe."—*Denton.*

A young father, finding his son with nothing to do, tore a map of the world out of a magazine, cut it up, and gave it to the boy to piece together again. A few minutes later the job was finished, and he asked his son how he ever did it so quickly.

"Well, Daddy," said the lad, "on the back of the map was a picture of a boy. I knew that if I could build the boy right, the world would come out right, too!"

—*Evangelical Visitor.*

It would be difficult to imagine that the babe under sentence of death, taken from the bulrush cradle by the daughter of Pharaoh, was destined to lead a nation from bondage to independence and establish a law that for ages was to remain the standard of justice and truth. Just as impossible a task would it be for a people of another and later age to believe that in a small back room of a low German saloon was born Martin Luther, one of the mightiest of the world's reformers, whose voice of thunder was to rock a world's foundation of a universal delusion. So it is just as impossible to know what may lie in the cradle of our homes!

Mother, as you rock your babe to and fro, soothing it with gentle murmur, or hushing it by lullaby, do you realize that in your arms of love you may clasp infinite possibilities, everlasting consequences, eternities of blessing or woe? So watch your treasure as the holy mother watched her firstborn. It is not of so much account whether the swaddling bands be composed of coarse linen or of fine cambric, the pillow of straw or of down; but it is of eternal importance to remember that early aspirations and inspirations infused into infant hearts give color and light for lifelong and eternal reflections, even as the sun gives the violet its hue and the buttercup its gold ere its budding.

. . . Don't wait until your child is of age before you introduce it to virtue. As soon as the natural eye can detect the shining of a star in the midnight sky, speak to it of what lies above and beyond. The stars will instruct the awakening intellect how virtue and truth shine all the brighter because of the dense darkness that covers the world's sorrow and sin.

There are cradle opportunities, though marked with poverty and limitations, that because of their seeming insignificance we regard with indifference, lose sight of, or abuse. Yet it is such beginnings that go to make up life; and, tiny as they seem, they are in reality great infinities, giving character to life, and shaping the soul for eternity. Surely nothing can be less than a magnitude, that contributes to a soul's eternal gain or loss!—Catherine Booth.

Where there is a really great man there was first a good mother.
—J. H. Jowett.

Someone asked a man of wisdom when the education of a child should be commenced. "Twenty years before his birth, by educating his mother," was the reply.—*Christian Advocate.*

> The sculptor, bending o'er his marble child,
> Models himself in fixed, enduring beauty;
> The painter's soul hath from the canvas smiled,
> Breathing deep tones of passion or of duty.
> —Anon.

CHAPTER IV

THE PREPARATION OF THE SCULPTRESS

When God wished for a mighty deliverer for His people, He began with a mother. On four different occasions in Scripture, God gave early intimation of the coming greatness of the child, so as to impress the sculptress with the importance of her task even before conception. Hence, with a sense of mission, the mother prepared first herself and then her child for the great task before him.

Frank Boreham has expressed part of this truth in this striking statement: "We fancy that God can only manage His world by big battalions abroad, when all the while He is doing it by beautiful babies at home. When a wrong wants righting, or a truth wants preaching, or a continent wants opening, God sends a baby into the world to do it. That is why, long, long ago, a Babe was born in Bethlehem."

It is natural for a young mother to prepare for the coming of her little one by making garments, preparing a nursery, and purchasing necessary equipment. How much more should she prepare herself and her home for the coming of a soul! In this beautiful poem, Fay Inchfawn has expressed this two-fold preparation:

MOTHER, I'M COMING

"I heard you, sweet! and I'll prepare,
So lovingly, your dainty wear.
Oh, I will dream and scheme each day,
And planning, put the pence away.
Then too, not only will I make
Soft, woolly comforts for your sake;
But I will fashion if I can,
Fine raiment for your inner man.
I will not think on evil things,
Lest I should clip my darling's wings.
I'll set my heart to understand
The great Salvation God has planned.

Yes, every atom of my being,
All feeling, tasting, hearing, seeing,
He shall refine, and garnish too.
I'll be God's woman through and through.
Lord, take me, and if this may be,
Possess my little child through me."

God, very evidently, planned that the knowledge of coming motherhood should draw a woman's soul to Himself. We have watched young, expectant mothers waiting in clinics for examinations, hurriedly herded from one room to another, more like cattle than molders of coming men and women. A little time taken with these young women, many of them unconverted, would count more than dozens of sermons from pulpits. How helpless many of them feel! A little friendly counsel on the greatness of their task and how to fulfil it by having the Christ-life implanted within, would be more welcome then than at other times.

Samson's parents longed for instruction after being told by the angel of the coming of their child. They prayed: "O my Lord, let the man of God which thou didst send come again unto us, and teach us what we shall do unto the child that shall be born." And when their prayer was heard and the angel returned, they asked, "How shall we order the child, and how shall we do for him?" This same request, we do not doubt, is the silent prayer that still arises in the hearts of parents-to-be in our generation.—E. & L. Harvey.

MOTHERHOOD

God gives a sweet, eternal gift to thee—
A little child to lead thee heavenward;
The clinging touch of fingers, satin-soft,
Reaches thy heart, and lifts it up to God.
God knows His gift will do the work He wills;
He clasps the child, knowing that mother hands
Will cling forever round a baby form,
And so both child and mother rest on God.

For baby's sake thou must live close to Him;
His soft eyes following thine must see His face.
Thy lips—those lips that press his unsoiled brow,
Must for his sake be pure and undefiled;
No false or foolish word, no angry tone,
Fall on the ear God formed to hear His voice.
Thou must remember that this budding soul
Will see his God in thee, and through thee—God.

Thy hands, caressing, helping, soothing him,
Must do no Christless thing. A mother's hand
Should be the saintliest hand in God's fair earth.
A mother's feet should shine with holiness,
For small, soft echoing steps tread after hers,
And oh, a mother's soul should radiant shine,
Crowned with a halo of celestial fire!

God has enriched her with the power to love,
And love should steep and soften heart and life;
A God-like love should prompt her daily rule,
Not blind to faults, but loving through them all
And chastening, knowing that her Holy Lord
Would not allow sin to sully child of His;
Solemn the mother's work, yet very sweet,
To picture to her children God in Christ.
—Eva I. Travers.

Give our boys better mothers, and they will give those mothers better sons.—Thomas Nelson.

The future state of the child depends in a great measure upon the home in which he is born. His soul is nourished and grows, above all, by the impressions which are there left upon his memory. My father gave me the example of sincerity carried even to scrupulousness, my mother, of a goodness rising to devotion the most heroic . . . I drank deep from my mother's mind; I read through her eyes; I felt through her impressions; I lived through her life.
—Lamartine.

I am much what my mother has made me.—Samuel Morley.

> The baby has no skies
> But mother's eyes;
> Nor any God above,
> But mother's love.
> His angel sees the Father's face,
> But he the mother's, full of grace;
> And yet the heavenly kingdom is of such as this.
> —John B. Tabb.

The benefits of motherhood are two-fold—if she is a true mother. Not only does she help to shape the soul and character of her child, but the mothering process does much to alter her. A striking analogy of this principle is to be found in the experience of the great sculptor, Michelangelo, as told by S. D. Gordon:

"When Michelangelo had finished his famous colossal statue of 'David, The Giant,' many of his friends who had not seen him during the years when he was working upon it in Florence, declared with great surprise that he was changed; his face was changed. And as they looked at the statue, and then at the skillful chiseler, it was seen that he had carved his conception of David, not only into the beautiful white stone, but all unconsciously he had carved it, too, into the lines of his own beautified, ennobled face."

MOTHER'S "INSPIRATION"

> Had I no little feet to guide
> Along life's toilsome way,
> My own more frequently might slide,
> More often go astray.
> But when I meet my baby's eyes,
> At God's own bar I stand,
> And angels draw me t'ward the skies
> While baby holds my hand.
> —McMaster.

If I were asked to name one principle that seemed to have an almost universal application, it would be this one—show me the mother and I will show you the man!—*Gleanings*.

Oliver Wendell Holmes said: "The real religion of the world comes from women much more than from men—from mothers most of all, who carry the key of our souls in their bosoms."

Thomas Carlyle said: "My dear mother, with the truthfulness of a mother's heart, ministered to all my wants, outward and inward, and even against hope, kept prophesying good . . . My kind mother did me one altogether invaluable service—she taught me, less indeed by word than by act and daily reverent look and habitude, her own simple version of the Christian faith . . . My mother, with a true woman's heart, and fine, though uncultivated sense, was in the strictest acceptation religious. The highest whom I knew on earth, I here saw bowed down with awe unspeakable before a Higher in Heaven; such things especially in infancy, reach inwards to the very core of your being."

Stories first heard at a mother's knee are never wholly forgotten—a little spring that dries not up in our journey through scorching years.

There are no men or women, however poor they may be, but have it in their power by the grace of God to leave behind them the grandest thing on earth, character; and their children might rise up after them and thank God that their mother was a pious woman, or their father a pious man.—Dr. McLeod.

No orator, no singer, no artist-worker, is to be compared with the mother who is carving the image of God in the soul of her little child. No mother need long to go out of the household, as if that were an obscure place. "The Gate of Heaven" is inscribed over every humble family.—Anon.

THE HAND THAT RULES THE WORLD

Infancy, the tender fountain,
    Ever may with beauty flow;
Mother's first to guide the streamlets;
    From them souls unresting grow—
Grow on for the good or evil,
    Sunshine streamed or darkness hurled;
For the hand that rocks the cradle
    Is the hand that rules the world.

Mother, how divine your mission
    Here upon our natal sod!
Keep, oh, keep the young heart open
    Always to the breath of God!
All true trophies of the ages
    Are from mother-love impearled,
For the hand that rocks the cradle
    Is the hand that rules the world.

"Blessings on the hand of mother!"
    Fathers, sons, and daughters cry,
And the sacred song is mingled
    With the worship in the sky—
Mingled where no tempest darkens,
    Rainbows ever gently curled;
For the hand that rocks the cradle
    Is the hand that rules the world.
                —Anon.

Dr. Campbell Morgan had four sons. They all became pastors. At a family renunion a friend asked one of the sons, "Which Morgan is the greatest preacher?"

The son looked at this father and promptly replied, "Mother!"
                —Unknown.

WHAT WE NEED

What does our country need? Not armies standing
    With sabers gleaming ready for the fight;
Not increased navies, skilful and commanding,
    To bound the waters with an iron might;
Not haughty men with glutted purses trying
    To purchase souls, and keep the power of place;
Not jeweled dolls with one another vying
    For palms of beauty, elegance, and grace.

But we want women, strong of soul, yet lowly,
    With that rare meekness, born of gentleness;
Women whose lives are pure, and clean, and holy,
    The women whom all little children bless;
Brave, earnest women, helpful to each other,
    With finest scorn for all things low and mean;
Women who hold the names of wife and mother
    Far nobler than the title of a queen.

Oh! these are they who mold the men of story,
    These mothers, ofttimes shorn of grace and youth,
Who, worn and weary, ask no greater glory
    Than making some young soul the home of truth;
Who sow in hearts all fallow for the sowing
    The seeds of virtue and of scorn for sin,
And, patient, watch the beauteous harvest growing
    And weed out tares which crafty hands cast in.

Women who do not hold the gift of beauty
    As some rare treasure to be bought and sold,
But guard it as a precious aid to duty—
    The outer framing of the inner gold;
Women who, low above their cradles bending,
    Let flattery's voice go by, and give no heed,
While their pure prayers like incense are ascending;
    These are our country's pride, our country's need.

—Ella Wheeler Wilcox.

Mothers, ye are the sculptors of the souls of the coming men; queens of the cradle, humble or high, ye are the queens of the future. In your hand lies the destinies of men. I am not speaking poetry, but plain fact, which history proves:

Nero's mother was a murderess; Nero was a murderer, on a gigantic scale.

Byron's mother was proud, ill-tempered, and violent; Byron was proud, ill-tempered, and violent.

Washington's mother was noble and pure; Washington was noble and pure.

Scott's mother loved poetry and painting; you know what Walter Scott was.

Carlyle's mother was stern and full of reverence; Carlyle was very much so.

Wesley's mother was a God-like woman; Wesley was a God-like man.

The prison chaplain will tell you that the last thing forgotten in all the recklessness of dissolute profligacy is the prayer or hymn taught by a mother's lips, or uttered to God at a father's knee. Yes, when all other roads are closed, there is one road open to the heart of the desperate man—the memory of his mother.—*Christian Treasury.*

CHAPTER V

MOTHER—SOUL SCULPTRESS

There is no nobler career than motherhood at its best. There are no possibilities greater than in being a mother, and in no other sphere does failure bring more serious penalties. With what diligence, then, should she prepare herself for such a task.

If the mechanic who is to work with "things" must study at a technical school, if the doctor into whose skilled hands will be entrusted human lives, must go through a medical school, if the teacher who is to help shape the human mind, must train at the university, how much more should the mother who is fashioning the souls of the men and women of tomorrow, learn at the highest of all schools and from the Master-Sculptor, Himself—God.

To attempt this task unprepared and untrained is tragic, and the results of doing so affect generations to come. On the other hand, there is no higher position to which humanity can aspire than that occupied by a converted, Heaven-inspired, praying mother.

—E. & L. Harvey.

The queen that sits upon the throne of home, crowned and sceptered as none other ever can be, is—mother. Her enthronement is complete, her reign is unrivaled, and the moral issues of her empire are eternal.—Anon.

> Mother, whoever you may be,
> You may think long and earnestly
> Of your high calling. Pondering
> The undreamed honor of the thing;
> Learning how God, through you, would plan
> To be well known to every man.
> And through your arms would gather fast
> The whole world to His heart at last.
> —Fay Inchfawn.

Peter Marshall, onetime Chaplain to the U. S. Senate, gives this warning to the women of America:

"The modern challenge to motherhood is the eternal challenge— that of being godly women. The very phrase sounds strange in our ears. We never hear it now.
"We hear about every other kind of women—
   beautiful women,
     smart women,
        sophisticated women,
           career women,
              talented women,
                 divorced women.
"But so seldom do we hear of a godly woman— or of a godly man either, for that matter.

"I believe women come nearer fulfilling their God-given function in the home than anywhere else.

"It is a much nobler thing to be a good wife than to be Miss America.

"It is a greater achievement to establish a Christian home than it is to produce a second-rate novel, filled with filth.

"It is a far, far better thing in the realms of morals to be old-fashioned than to be ultramodern.

"The world has enough women who know how to hold their cocktails, who have lost all their illusions and their faith.

"The world has enough women who know how to be smart.
   It needs women who are willing to be simple.
The world has enough women who know how to be brilliant.
   It needs some who will be brave.
The world has enough women who are popular.
   It needs more who are pure.
We need women, and men, too, who would rather
   be morally right than socially correct.

"Let us not fool ourselves—without Christianity, without Christian education, without the principles of Christ inculcated into young life, we are simply rearing pagans.

"Physically, they will be perfect. Intellectually, they will be brilliant. But spiritually, they will be pagan. Let us not fool ourselves.

"The twentieth century challenge to motherhood—when it is all boiled down—is that mothers will have an experience of God . . . a reality which they can pass on to their children." (From his book of sermons, *Mr. Jones, Meet the Master*, Peter Davies, Ltd.).

Oh, Mothers of young children, I bow before you in reverence. Your work is most holy. You are fashioning the destinies of immortal souls. The powers folded up in the little ones that you hushed to sleep in your bosoms last night, are powers that shall exist for ever. You are preparing them for their immortal destiny and influence. Be faithful. Take up your sacred burden reverently. Be sure that your heart is pure and that your life is sweet and clean.

The Persian apologue says that the lump of clay was fragrant because it had lain on a rose. Let your life be as the rose, and then your child, as it lies upon your bosom, will absorb the fragrance. If there is no sweetness in the rose, the clay will not be perfumed.

—J. R. Miller.

A MOTHER'S TRUST

Beneath the bloodstained lintel I with my children stand;
A messenger of judgment is passing through the land;
There is no other refuge from the destroyer's face—
Beneath the bloodstained lintel shall be our hiding-place.

The Lamb of God has suffered, our sins and griefs He bore;
By faith the blood is sprinkled above our dwelling's door.
The Lord, Who judges righteously, has given that sacred sign;
Tonight the bloodstained lintel shall shelter me and mine.

My Savior, for my dear ones, I claim Thy promise true;
The Lamb is "for the household"—the children's Savior too.
On earth the little children once felt Thy touch divine;
Beneath the bloodstained lintel—Thy blessing give to mine.

O Thou Who gavest, guard them—those wayward little feet,
The wilderness before them, the ills of life to meet.
My mother-love is helpless, I trust them to Thy care!
Beneath the bloodstained lintel—my place is ever there.

The faith I rest upon Thee, Thou wilt not disappoint;
With wisdom, Lord, to train them, my shrinking heart anoint.
With all my children, Father, I then shall see Thy face—
Under the bloodstained lintel—the token of Thy grace.

O wonderful Redeemer, Who suffered for our sake,
When o'er the guilty nations the judgment storm shall break,
With joy from that safe shelter, may we then meet Thine eye,
Beneath the bloodstained lintel, my children, Lord, and I.

—Anon.

 A mother at prayer and Bible study, is simply a mother in the presence of the great Master-Sculptor, receiving instructions and strength and calm for the daily tasks. Such mothers who feel indebted to Christ for their own salvation and who daily converse with Him, keeping spiritual values uppermost, are bound to esteem for their children the service of Christ rather than any other earthly career.

 Great alarm is expressed today at the fast diminishing number of young men coming forward as candidates for the ministry and mission-field. We work at great disadvantage if we endeavor to move young men in this direction whose characters have already been shaped and molded so that they value money-making and popular careers above the honor of being a follower of Jesus Christ. Let us rather pray earnestly for an old-fashioned revival of praying mothers. A great authority has called the mother the Church's principal recruiting officer.

J. R. Mott, missionary, preacher, and youth authority, said:

"A few years ago I made a somewhat extensive study of the factors and influences entering into the decisions of several thousand men who had decided to become ministers. This study was supplemented by reviewing the biographies of several hundred leading ministers of various communions. Both studies indicated that the mothers had been, up to that time, the principal influence to which these men attributed their decision."

On the same subject, Theodore Cuyler had this to say:

"When I was a student in Princeton, the chairman of the examining board requested all who had praying mothers to rise. Nearly a hundred and fifty leaped to their feet. There we stood, living witnesses to the power of a mother's prayers, and of her shaping influence and example. My own widowed mother was one of the best that God ever gave an only son . . . If all mothers were like her, the 'church in the house' would be one of the best feeders of the church in the sanctuary."

Dr. Talmage tells us that, on one occasion, when 120 clergymen were gathered together, they began to compare experiences, and it was found that 100 out of the 120 assigned as the instrumentality of their conversion a Christian mother.

Such praying mothers had the indomitable spirit that would conquer all through prayer. An unknown author has peeped behind the scenes and given us a beautiful picture of just such a mother:

MOTHER'S ELBOWS ON MY BED

"I was but a youth and thoughtless,
    As all youths are apt to be;
Though I had a Christian mother
    Who had taught me carefully.
But there came a time when pleasure
    Of the world came to allure,
And I no more sought the guidance
    Of her love so good and pure.

"Her tender admonitions fell
    But lightly on my ear,
And for the gentle warnings
    I felt an inward sneer.
How could I prove my manhood
    Were I not firm of will?
No threat of future evil
    Should all my pleasure kill.

"But mother would not yield her boy
    To Satan's sinful sway,
And though I spurned her counsel
    She knew a better way.
No more she tried to caution
    Of ways she knew were vain,
And though I guessed her heartache
    I could not know its pain.

"She made my room an altar,
    A place of secret prayer,
And there she took her burden
    And left it in His care.
And morning, noon, and evening
    By that humble bedside low,
She sought the aid of Him Who
    Best can understand a mother's woe.

"And I went my way unheeding,
    Careless of the life I led,
Until one day I noticed
    Prints of elbows on my bed.
Then I saw that she had been there
    Praying for her wayward boy,
Who for love of worldly pleasure
    Would her peace of mind destroy.

"While I wrestled with my conscience,
    Mother wrestled still in prayer,
Till that little room seemed hallowed
    Because so oft she met Him there.

With her God she held the fortress,
    And though not a word she said,
My stubborn heart was broken
    By those imprints on my bed.

"Long the conflict raged within me,
    Sin against my mother's prayers.
Sin MUST YIELD for MOTHER NEVER
    While she daily met Him there.
And her constant love and patience
    Were like coals upon my head,
Together with the imprints
    Of her elbows on my bed.

"Mother-love and God-love
    Are a combination rare,
And one that can't be beaten
    When sealed by earnest prayer.
And so at last the fight was won,
    And I to Christ was led,
And mother's prayers were answered
    By her elbows on my bed."

Many will have heard of the well-known poet and hymn-writer, Horatius Bonar, and of his spiritually-minded brother, Andrew, who wrote the life of Robert M. McCheyne. Of the seven Bonar brothers, three became eminent ministers of the Free Church of Scotland. What shaped these godly men for such spheres of usefulness? Part of the secret might be found in the godly example of their widowed mother. In a diary entry by Andrew at her death, we read:

"I never forget the firmness and regularity with which she kept to herself the morning hour for being alone after breakfast, and the hour before evening worship. This struck me when a boy."

Charles Inwood, a Keswick speaker and well-known evangelist, had a mother who excelled in the hidden ministry of prayer. His biographer says: "Certain it is that she dedicated before birth her firstborn, Charles, to the Lord. And to her prayers as much as to her husband's zeal and example, must be ascribed the fact that of five sons, four dedicated themselves to the ministry."

We would have more mothers such as these if their heart-cry were voiced in these words of Louise B. Eavey:

> "Dear Lord, I bring to Thee my son
> Whose tender years have scarce begun.
> In this wee frame I know full well
> A living soul has come to dwell
> Who needs Thee now at childhood's gate,
> Ere he shall grow to man's estate.
> I covenant through hours apart
> To pray for him with fervent heart,
> To teach Thy Word with winsome voice
> By day and night until his choice
> Be but Thy blood for sin's deep stain,
> And my small son is born again.
> Then onward shall I pray the more
> And teach Thy precepts o'er and o'er,
> That he may grow, each boyhood hour,
> By Thine indwelling, risen power.
> Lord, some small boys with none to care
> Will never hear a mother's prayer;
> Prepare my son with love aflame
> To reach them with Thy saving name.
> And make him, Lord, a polished tool,
> A learner in Thy highest school.
> A mother's part seems, oh, so frail!
> But Thy strong arm can never fail.
> To teach, to pray, to stand are mine;
> The miracles must all be Thine.
> Expectantly I yield to Thee
> The little boy Thou gavest me."

Peter Marshall could well have echoed the Scottish proverb, "An ounce of mother is worth more than a pound of clergy," for he had a wonderful mother. As he left home for his first job, she turned to him at the little iron gate and gave this advice: "Dinna forget your verse, my laddie, 'Seek ye first the kingdom of God and his righteousness, and all these things shall be added unto you.' Long ago I pit ye in the Lord's hands, and I'll no be takin' ye awa noo. He will tak' care o' you. Dinna worry."

A mother of eight children many years ago made this simple record: "This morning I rose early to pray for my children, and especially that my sons may be ministers and missionaries of Jesus Christ." This prayer was answered and five of her sons became ministers and missionaries of Jesus Christ. This was the well-known Beecher family.

Samuel Zwemer, missionary authority on Moslems, came from a home where all major decisions were made after seasons of prayer. Fellowship with Christ was enjoyed three times a day after each meal, as the family gathered around the Word and in prayer. Of the five brothers, four entered the Christian ministry, and sister Nellie spent forty years in China.—E. & L. Harvey.

> The sweetest sound heard through our earthly home,
> The brightest ray that gleams from Heaven's dome,
> The loveliest flower that e'er from earth's breast rose,
> The purest flame that, quivering, gleams and glows—
> Are found alone where kneels a mother mild,
> With heart uplifted, praying for her child.
> —Anon.

The ablest theological professor is a Christian mother, who, out of her own experience, can tell the four-year-old how beautiful Christ was on earth, and how beautiful He now is in Heaven, and how dearly He loves little folks. And then she kneels down and puts one arm around the boy, and with her somewhat faded cheek against the roseate cheek of the little one, consecrates him for time and eternity to Him who said, "Suffer little children to come unto me."
—Talmage.

I believe I should have been swept away by the flood of French infidelity, if it had not been for one thing—the remembrance of the time when my sainted mother used to make me kneel by her side, taking my little hands folded in hers, and caused me to repeat the Lord's prayer.—Randolph.

MY MOTHER'S VOICE

My mother's voice!—how does it creep
    In cadence on my lonely hours;
Like healing sent on wings of sleep,
    Or dew upon th' unconscious flowers.

I might forget her melting prayer
    While pleasure's pulses madly fly;
But in the still, unbroken air,
    Her gentle tones come stealing by.
And years of sin and manhood flee,
And leave me at my mother's knee.
        —Unkown.

AT MOTHER'S KNEE

The fire upon the hearth is low,
    And there is stillness everywhere;
    Like troubled spirits, here and there
The firelight shadows fluttering go.
And as the shadows 'round me creep,
    A childish treble breaks the gloom,
    And softly from a farther room
Comes: "Now I lay me down to sleep."

And somehow, with that little prayer
    And that sweet treble in my ears,
    My thought goes back to distant years
And lingers with a dear one there;
And, as I hear the child's "Amen,"
    My mother's faith comes back to me,
    Couched at her side I seem to be,
And mother holds my hands again.

O for an hour in that dear place!
    O for the peace of that dear time!
    O for that childish trust sublime!
O for a glimpse of mother's face!
Yet, as the shadows 'round me creep,
    I do not seem to be alone:
    Sweet magic of that treble tone—
And, "Now I lay me down to sleep."
        —Unkown.

WHO CAMPS TONIGHT?

Shall I tell you about the battle
    That was fought in the world today,
Where thousands went down like heroes
    To death in the pitiless fray?

You may know someone of the wounded
    And some of the fallen when
I tell you this wonderful battle
    Was fought in the hearts of men.

Not with the sounding of trumpets,
    Nor clashing of sabers drawn,
But silent as twilight in Autumn,
    All day the fight went on.

And over against temptation
    A mother's prayers were cast
That had come by silent marches
    From the lullaby land of the past.

And over the field of battle
    The force of ambition went,
Driving before it, like arrows,
    The children of sweet content.

And memories odd and olden
    Came up through the dust of years,
And hopes that were glad and golden
    Were met by a host of fears.

And the hearts grew worn and weary,
    And said, "Oh, can it be
That I am worth the struggle
    You are making today for me?"

For the heart itself was the trophy
    And prize of this wavering fight!
And tell me, O gentle reader,
    "Who camps on the field tonight?"
              —Unknown.

Just a few years before the birth of John Wesley, his mother made a resolution to spend one hour, morning and evening, in prayer and meditation. This she kept unless sickness hindered, and if opportunity offered she spent some time at noon as well. To mothers of modern days who claim they are too busy, we might explain that Mrs. Wesley was the mother of nineteen children and was their teacher as well.—E. & L. Harvey.

TOO-BUSY MOTHER

"I'd take the time, dear Lord, to pray,
But see what work there is today—
The washing, baking, clothes to mend,
And all the family to tend."
And so goes by another day
Without a moment spent to pray.

Things go awry, the starch boils o'er;
My temper's high—I mop the floor—
The rush to do my work aright
Does not seem worth the fight by night.
Perhaps I would accomplish more
If strength and grace were gained before!

"Forgive me, Lord, the 'Martha view,'
When I so need the time with You.
I'm sure a quarter-hour or so
Would help to rout my own soul's foe.
I cannot be from care set free
Without some fellowship with Thee."
—Frances R. Longing.

Billy Sunday tells the story of a minister who was making calls. When he rang the bell of a certain home, a little girl opened the door. He asked for her mother, and she asked, "Are you sick?"

He said he wasn't, and she asked, "Are you hurt?"

Again he said, "No."

Then she asked if he knew of anyone sick or injured. When he replied that he did not, she said, "Then you can't see mama, for she prays from nine to ten o'clock."

It was then twenty minutes after nine, but the minister sat down and waited for forty minutes to see her. At ten o'clock she came in with the light of glory on her face, and he knew why that home was so bright; he knew why her two sons were in theological seminary and her daughter was a missionary. All hell cannot tear a boy or girl away from a mother like that.—*Fellowship News.*

Short Tributes from Successful Men

I remember my mother's prayers—and they have always followed me. They have clung to me all my life.—Abraham Lincoln.

If I am Thy child, Only God, it is because Thou gavest me such a mother.—St. Augustine.

Nothing can ever make my mother's memory other than the greatest gift I ever received!—Dean Stanley.

The happiest part of my happy life has been my mother.
—Washington Irving.

All that I have ever accomplished in my life I owe to my mother.
—D. L. Moody.

The influence of a good mother is worth more than a thousand schoolmasters.—George Herbert.

> A mother is a mother still,
> The holiest thing alive.—Coleridge.

Humanly speaking, my mother is the author of my ministry. When I was born, she consecrated me to God and prayed that I might be a minister of the Gospel. My first memory was sitting on her knee, as a little child, as she taught me the text, "God so loved the world!"—Newman Hall, D.D.

The famous revivalist, Edward Payson, wrote in a letter to his mother: "To your admonitions and instructions I am indebted for all the moral and religious impressions which are imprinted on my mind, and which I hope will give me reason to bless you through all eternity."

The need today is for mothers with a godly purpose, to whom the thought of seeing their children's lives marred by sin and Satan is unthinkable. Such a one was Charles H. Spurgeon's mother. When we think of the souls he won, the sermons he preached, the young men he trained, the institutions he left behind—we look for the cause. We have not far to seek when we read this stirring challenge from this mother-sculptress:

"I have trained you in righteousness. Your father and I have set you right examples. We have taught you the Gospel. We have shown you the way of peace. My son, if you do not live a godly life, I will stand before God in the day of judgment and bear witness against you."

WHEN MOTHER PRAYED

I think that I shall never see,
This side of God's eternity,
A scene as lovely as the one
Which met my gaze when day was done,
In childhood years of long ago.

My mother sang, 'twas sweet and low,
Her face with love was all aglow;
She turned the pages of God's Word;
Her tender heart was deeply stirred.

She knelt, she prayed, oh, what a prayer!
I listened, lingering on the stair.
"God bless my boy"—I heard my name—
And there, within my heart, a flame
Began to burn, 'tis burning yet.
That hour I shall not forget!

Though mother dear no longer kneels
And prays for me, this night there steals
A ray of warmth into my heart.
And now, like her, from cares apart,

I pray. Her prayers still follow me—
A torch—and by its gleam I see
My home across the crystal sea.
—David F. Nygren.

A mother took alone the burden of life when her husband laid it down. Without much property, out of her penury, by her planning and industry night and day, by her willfulness of love, by her fidelity, she brought up her children. And life has six men, all of whom are like pillars in the temple of God. And, oh, do not read to me of the campaigns of Caesar; tell me nothing about Napoleon's wonderful exploits. I tell you that, as God and the angels look down upon the silent history of that woman's administration, and upon those men-building processes which went on in her heart and mind through a score of years, nothing exterior, no outward development of kingdoms, no empire building, can compare with what she has done. Nothing can compare in beauty and wonder and admirableness to the silent work in obscure dwellings of faithful women bringing up their children to honor and virtue and piety.—H. W. Beecher.

THE BRAVEST BATTLE

The bravest battle that ever was fought!
Shall I tell you where and when?
On the maps of the world you will find it not.
'Twas fought by the mothers of men.
Nay, not with cannon or battle shot,
With a sword or noble pen;
Nay, not with eloquent words or thought
From mouths of wonderful men!

But deep in a walled-up woman's heart—
Of a woman that would not yield,
But bravely, silently bore her part—
So, there is that battlefield!
No marshaling troops, no bivouac song,
No banner to gleam and wave;
But oh! these battles—they last so long,
From babyhood to the grave.
—Joaquin Miller.

J. Wilbur Chapman nodded courteously and tipped his hat to a neighbor and his wife. Chapman's little boy did the same thing with heart-touching gravity. The neighbor reined up the horse, roared with laughter, and said, "Have the little fellow do it again!"

Chapman's eyes filled with tears. "Oh, my friend, it is serious with me. He is watching everything I do."—*Cross and Crown.*

"And Solomon loved the Lord, walking in the statutes of David his father" (I Kings 3:3).

CHAPTER VI

FATHER AS SCULPTOR

Many a sermon has been preached to mothers; many a tract and treatise written on mother's influence. But how often are sermons preached to fathers? Is there any power for good or evil greater than the influence of him who leads the family, who propagates his own character in the persons and the souls of his children, who lives his own life over again in the lives of those whom he has begotten?

Like father, like family; set this down as a philosophical principle. Occasional exceptions do not undermine the rule; it is an organic one. The father impresses himself upon his children just as undesignedly, but as surely as I impress my shadow on the ground when I walk into the sunshine. The father cannot help it if he would. The father leads by God's decree. He makes the home laws, fixes the precedents, creates the home atmosphere, and the "odor of the house" clings to the garments of the children, if they go around the globe. "He is a chip off the old block," said someone when he heard the younger Pitt's first speech. "Nay," replied Burke, "he is the old block himself."

. . . A father's devoted godliness is often reproduced in his children, but still oftener are his errors and his vices. He commonly sets the habits of the household. Whatever "fires the father kindles, the children gather the wood." If the father rises late on the Sabbath morning, the boys come down late and ill-humored to the table. If he goes on a Sunday excursion, they must carry the lunch and the fishing tackle, and share in the guilty sport.

In looking over my congregation, I find that, while several pious fathers have unconverted children, there are but few prayerless fathers who have converted sons. The pull of the father downward is too strong for the upward pull of the Sabbath School and the pulpit. If the father talks money constantly, he usually rears a family for Mammon. If he talks pictures and books at his table, he is likely to awaken a thirst for literature or art. If he talks horses, games, and prizefights, he brings up a family of jockeys and sportsmen. If he makes his own fireside attractive in the evening, he will probably succeed in anchoring his children at home. But if he hears the clock strike eleven in the theatre or the clubhouse, he need not be surprised if his boys hear it strike twelve in the gambling-den or the public-house. If he leads in irreligion, what but the grace of God can keep his imitative household from following him to perdition? The history of such a family is commonly written in that sadly frequent description given in the Old Testament —"He walked in all the sins of his father" (1 Kings 15:3).—Theodore Cuyler.

TO ANY LITTLE BOY'S FATHER

There are little eyes upon you,
    And they're watching night and day;
There are little ears that quickly
    Take in every word you say.
There are little hands all eager
    To do everything you do,
And a little boy who's dreaming
    Of the day he'll be like you.

You're the little fellow's hero;
    You're the wisest of the wise;
In his little mind, about you,
    No suspicions ever rise.
He believes in you devoutly,
    Holds that all you say and do,
He will say and do in your way
    When he's grown up just like you.

There's a wide-eyed little fellow,
    Who believes you're always right;
And his ears are always open
    And he watches day and night.
You are setting an example
    Every day in all you do,
For the little boy who's waiting
    To grow up to be like you!
                —Selected.

The most casual observer recognizes the tendency of a small boy to imitate his father. A policeman's son must have a uniform with brass buttons. A child of a truck driver is only happy with a toy motor. A carpenter's son would be forever driving nails with a toy hammer or sawing into some favorite piece of furniture. A child brought up on a farm wants to have chicks of his own or rear a pet calf. The wee fellow whose father is a sailor can think of nothing but boats.

A father's hobbies and even mannerisms likewise become the subject of imitation. We smile at these, and often the father is proud to call the attention of his friends to this miniature copy of himself. But what he usually fails to see is that his vices and sins will just as readily be reproduced in the innocent little imitator. "He did according to all things as Joash his father did" (II Kings 14:3).

—E. & L. Harvey.

"Is it well with the child?" (II Kings 4:26)

"I'M STEPPING IN YOUR STEPS!"

Climbing the mountain wild and high,
    Bold was the glance of his eagle eye,
Proud was the spirit that knew no fear,
    Reckless the tread of the mountaineer.

Up and up through the fields of snow,
    Down and down o'er the rocks below,
On and on o'er the pathway steep,
    On o'er the chasms wide and deep.

Hark! O'er the mountain bleak and wild
    Echoed the voice of a little child:
"Papa, look out! I am coming, too,
    Stepping in your steps, just like you.

"Papa, O Papa! Just see me,
    Walking like Papa—don't you see?"
Pale was the cheek of the mountaineer—
    Pale with the thrill of an awful fear.

Paused he quick, and with eager face,
    Clasped the child in his strong embrace;
Backward glanced, with his eye so dim,
    Back o'er the path he had followed him.

Father, pause in the path of life,
    Rough with the chasms of sin and strife;
When you walk with a step so free
    'Mong the rocks where the dangers be,

List to the voice that is sounding sweet,
    List! They are coming—the little feet!
Walk with care; they are coming too,
    "Stepping in your steps, just like you."
                      —Mrs. Avery Stuttle.

    To children, a father is a flesh-and-blood example of manhood. It is from him that a young girl derives a sense of what a man does, stands for, opposes, believes. His example will for ever determine her responses to men. Similarly, the male child, even in his cot, begins to apprehend from his father the early bits and parts of what he is expected to become. If father "isn't there" the youthful mind will be at a loss, for there will be no example upon which to act, or from which to react. The absence of a father leaves a vast, inner desert, a guideless anxiety. Slowly there arises in the young mind a sense of having been let down. His father makes him feel rejected simply by being too busy or too tired for active companionship.

    Is this neglect necessary, even for a hard-working father? There are 168 hours in a week. The average man spends about 44 of them at work. Allow another 15 hours for traveling time, lunch, overtime, etc. Then set aside 56 hours, eight each night, for sleep. That adds up to 115 hours—leaving Dad 53 hours for eating, relaxing, or whatever he wants to do. Surely in those 53 hours he could find time to be a father to his children?

But does he do it? By and large, no. Mother tries to teach her sons to become men. But she can no more represent all that a man ought to be than a canary can teach a goldfish the joys, duties, and problems of living under water.

Fatherhood not only means love, integrity, courage, knowledge, and a good balance of faith and skepticism; it also means sharing those qualities day by day with the people who depend on them for the future—children, that is. Obviously, Dad can't be a real father if he is not at home—in mind and heart and spirit, as well as in body.

But Dad has left home. He won't come back until it dawns on him that the most profound satisfactions in his life arise from being a father first, and only after that a first-class sportsman or a big noise in business.—Philip Wylie.

(Reproduced by permission of The Readers' Digest Association, Ltd., British Edition, April 1956).

WANTED: A MAN TO LEAD

There isn't a boy but wants to grow
    Manly and true at heart,
And every lad would like to know
    The secrets we can impart.
He doesn't want to slack or shirk—
    Oh, haven't you heard him plead?
He'll follow a man at play or work
    If only the man will lead.

Where are the men to lead today,
    Sparing an hour or two,
Teaching the boy the game to play,
    Just as a man should do?
Village and slums are calling—"Come,
    Here are the boys!" Indeed,
Who can tell what they might become
    If only the man would lead.

> Where are the men to lend a hand?
> Echo it far and wide—
> Men who will rise in every land,
> Bridging the "Great Divide."
> Nation and flag and tongue unite
> Joining each class and creed.
> Here are the boys who would do right—
> But where are the men to lead?
> —*Wesleyan Methodist.*

"And ye fathers . . . bring them up in the nurture and admonition of the Lord" (Eph. 6: 4).

The father is more than a mere example. He is the head of the home in the truest sense of the word (Eph. 5:23). A home without a head would be like a country without a government; anarchy would be the result. Child delinquency and many of our other national evils spring from the chaos that exists in thousands of homes where the father fails in this function. We get a little picture in Paul's epistle to Timothy of God's view of what a father should be in the home. One of the chief requisites for any officer in the church was that he be "one that ruleth well his own house, having his children in subjection with all gravity" (I Tim. 3:4).

Even the ancient pagan Greeks recognized a father's responsibility. Plato, the ancient philosopher, could have taught something to our modern juvenile courts of today. Seeing a child in mischief, Plato punished the father, thus dealing with the trouble at its source.

We laugh at the Victorian "tyranny" in the home, and while we recognize that it was often carried much too far, we today are in much greater danger from the appalling landslide in the opposite direction. We read recently of parents who wrote to a teacher objecting to the punishment of their child. "We never punish or hit him except in self-defense," was their surprising admission.

The wisest man that ever lived, Solomon, has given us more directives on the much disputed subject of corporal punishment: "Foolishness is bound in the heart of a child; but the rod of correction shall drive it far from him" (Prov. 22: 15). And yet, we moderns claim to be wiser than the wisest man to the undoing of ourselves and our offspring. Other words of wisdom could be found from this same source in Prov. 13: 24; Prov. 19: 18; and Prov. 23: 13.

—E. & L. Harvey.

A lecturer recently declared, in beginning his lecture, that he had received his moral training "at the knee of a devoted mother and across the knee of a determined father." One wonders how many of the oncoming generation will be able to make such a statement."

—*Christian Work.*

MY PRAYER

Father, today I bring to Thee
    This boy of mine whom Thou hast made.
In everything he looks to me;
    In turn, I look to Thee for aid.

He knows not all that is before;
    He little dreams of hidden snares.
He holds my hand, and o'er and o'er
    I find myself beset with fears.

Father, as this boy looks to me
    For guidance, and my help implores,
I bring him now in prayer to Thee;
    He trusts my strength, and I trust Yours.

Hold Thou my hand as I hold his,
    And so guide me that I may guide.
Teach me, Lord, that I may teach,
    And keep me free from foolish pride.

Help me to help this boy of mine,
    To be to him a father true.
Hold me, Lord for everything
    As fast as I hold my boy for You.

—Nauzon W. Brapham.

The father is the head of the home, with gentle dignity acting his full part as head. He is the priest and minister to his household. The simple word of thanksgiving at the meal, the gathering of the family together, morning or night or both, for reading a bit out of the old Book of God, and in simplest, homeliest language, giving thanks and asking a blessing upon the circle—these belong to the father. They are a part of the simple meaning of the word "father." For a father is a priest or minister. He was a father before he was a priest, and only became priest because he was a father. . . .

With the mother, he is in his home the teacher of the school, the consulting librarian of the book world, the president of the literary society and of the social club, and the chief craftsman of the workshop.—S. D. Gordon.

WHEN FATHER PRAYS

When father prays he doesn't use
    The words the preacher does;
There's different things for different days—
    But mostly it's for us.
When father prays the house is still,
    His voice is slow and deep.
We shut our eyes, the clock ticks loud,
    So quiet we must keep.
He prays that we may be good boys,
    And later on, good men;
And then we squirm, and think we won't
    Have any quarrels again.
You'd never think to look at Dad,
    He once had tempers too.
I guess if father needs to pray,
    We youngsters surely do.
Sometimes the prayer gets very long
    And hard to understand,
And then I wiggle up quite close,
    And let him hold my hand.
I can't remember all of it—
    I'm little yet, you see;
But one thing I cannot forget—
    My father prays for me.
                  —Selected.

A well-known evangelist, Gypsy Smith, had this to say about praying fathers: "In four English-speaking countries, I have been for a quarter of a century trying to deal with men and women and children, and oh, how many boys and girls have come to me and said, when life had become ruined for them, 'Ah, Mr. Smith, my life would have been different if my father had prayed, but I have not had a praying father, and that makes a difference.'"

Two fathers in Bible times voiced a concern for their sons in the form of questions:
"What shall I do for my son?" (I Sam. 10:2).
"Is the young man Absalom safe?" (II Sam. 18:32).

"I understood the loving fatherhood of God as Jesus taught it," said the godly Samuel Zwemer, "because of what I saw in my own father."

A FATHER'S PRAYER

Lord, strengthen me that I may be
    A fit example for my son.
Grant he may never hear or see
    A shameful deed that I have done.
How ever sorely I am tried,
Let me not undermine his pride.

Lord, make me tolerant and wise,
    Incline my ears to hear him through.
Let him not stand with downcast eyes
    Fearing to trust me and be true.
Instruct me so that I may know
The way my son and I should go.

When he shall err as once I did,
    Or boyhood's folly bids him stray,
Let me not into anger fly
    And drive the good in him away.
Teach me to win his trust—that he
Shall keep no secret hid from me.

Lord, as his father now I pray
    For manhood's strength and counsel wise.
Let me deal justly day by day,
    In all that fatherhood implies.
To be his father, keep me fit,
Let me not play the hypocrite.

("A Father's Prayer" is from the book *Light of Faith* by Edgar Guest. Copyright 1926. The Reilly & Lee Co., Chicago, Ill., U.S.A.)

What better reward at the end of life than to receive a tribute such as this:

FATHER OF MINE !

"Father of mine, some years ago
You showed me the way I ought to go;
You led my feet past the treach'rous sand
By the gentle clasp of your own strong hand.

"Father of mine, let me thank you for
The prayers you prayed and the burden you bore.
Like a guiding star thro' the tempests' strife,
All your precepts have shone on my path of life.

"Father of mine, when the time has passed
And the work of my life is complete at last,
When I step ashore on the glory strand
With a grateful heart I will clasp your hand."
—Sarah K. Marine.

(Copyright by Lillenas Publishing Co., U.S.A.)

God's purpose in sending a little one to the home is twofold. He not only seeks a parent to train the child, but He often uses the child to beckon the parent back to all that is good and pure—back to Himself.

THE CHAP AT HOME

To feel his little hand in mine,
    So clinging and so warm,
To know he thinks me strong enough
    To keep him safe from harm;
To see his simple faith in all
    That I can say or do;

It sort o' shames a fellow,
    But it makes him better, too.
And I'm trying hard to be the man
    He fancies me to be,
Because I have this chap at home
    Who thinks the world of me.

I would not disappoint his trust
    For anything on earth,
Nor let him know how little I
    Just naturally am worth.
But after all, it's easier
    That brighter road to climb,
With the little hands behind me
    To push me all the time.
And I reckon I'm a better man
    Than what I used to be
Because I have this chap at home
    Who thinks the world of me.
              —Selected.

THE TWO PRAYERS

Last night my little boy
    Confessed to me
Some childish wrong;
    And kneeling at my knee
He prayed with tears:
    "Dear God, make me a man
Like Daddy—wise and strong;
    I know You can."

Then while he slept
    I knelt beside his bed,
Confessed my sins,
    And prayed with low-bowed head:
"O God, make me a child,
    Like my child here—
Pure, guileless,
    Trusting Thee with faith sincere."
          —*Sunday School Times.*

"Fathers, provoke not your children to anger" (Col. 3: 21).

THE HEART OF HOME

Lord, let our house be something more
Than just a shelter with a door;
    May its windows glow with light,
    Shedding radiance through the night.
Not just a glitter of glass and chrome,
But give it the "feel" of a happy home.

Let it have flowers, a well-loved book,
Soft cushions in a quiet nook.
    May it be more than downy bed,
    Or snowy cloth with silver spread;
Lend it some smiles, warm sympathy,
With kindly thoughts, true charity—
    That all may recall, though far they roam,
    That God was there—in the heart of home.
                —Christine White.

CHAPTER VII

HOME—THE WORKSHOP

A music-lover desired to see the factory where lovely pianos were turned out. But within, all seemed confusion to him; the din was deafening. Strewn here and there were pieces of various materials. He who had been accustomed to hearing beautiful strains from a finished instrument could hardly reconcile the seemingly meaningless hammering, and the shapeless, unpolished bits and pieces. The visitor expected something of a showroom display, but the skilled workmen, with a vision in mind, saw purpose in the seeming chaos.

Do we try to make our homes showrooms before they have been workshops? If the principal task of mother and father is sculpturing, will not our homes be equipped and furnished with this in mind? A parent cannot at the same time be house-proud and task-conscious. A mother must be willing to brave the criticisms of friends who do not share her vision. Her home must be a haven for her children rather than a showroom for admiring friends.

Many a delinquent or atheist today could trace the beginning of his misdeeds and unbelief to the absence of a real home. I wonder if your boy could voice his complaints in the following sentiments:

NO PLACE FOR BOYS

"What can a boy do, and where can a boy stay,
If he is always told to get out of the way?

"He cannot sit here, and he must not stand there.
The cushions that cover that overstuffed chair
Were put there, of course, to be seen and admired;
A boy has no business to ever feel tired.
The beautiful roses and flowers that bloom
On the floor of the darkened and delicate room
Were not made to walk on—at least not by boys.
The house is no place, anyway, for their noise.

"Yet boys must walk somewhere and what if their feet,
Sent out of our houses, sent into the street,
Should step round the corner, and pause at the door
Where other boys' feet have paused often before?
Should pass through the gateway of glittering light
Where jokes that are merry and songs that are bright
Ring out a warm welcome with flattering voice,
And temptingly say, 'Here's a place for you boys!'

"Ah, what if they should? What if your boy or mine
Should cross o'er the threshold which marks out the line
'Twixt virtue and vice, 'twixt pureness and sin,
And leave all his innocent boyhood within?
O! what if they should, because you and I,
While the days and the months and the years hurry by,
Are too busy with cares and with life's fleeting joys
To make 'round our hearthstone a place for the boys?

"There's a place for the boys; they'll find it somewhere,
And if our own homes are too daintily fair
For the touch of their fingers, or the tread of their feet,
They'll find it, and find it alas, in the street
'Mid the gildings of sin and the glitter of vice.
With the heartaches and longings, we pay a dear price
For the getting of gain that our lifetime employs,
If we fail to provide a good place for the boys."
—Unknown.

The temptation to bestow all our time and attention on the home at the expense of soul-sculpturing is here aptly set forth in this searching quotation:

"I am sadly concerned that thousands of mothers are so overburdened that the actual demands of life from day to day consume all their time and strength. But of two evils, choose the lesser. And which would you call the lesser, an unpolished stove or an untaught boy? Dirty windows, or a child whose confidence you have failed to gain? Cobwebs in the corner, or a son over whose soul a crust has formed so strong that you despair of melting it with your hot tears and your fervent prayers?

"I have seen a woman who was absolutely ignorant of her children's habits of thought, who never felt that she could spare a half-hour to read or talk with them—I have seen this woman spend ten minutes in ironing a sheet, or forty minutes in icing a cake for tea because company was expected.

"When the mother, a good orthodox Christian, shall appear before the Great White Throne, to be judged for 'the deeds done in the body,' and to give in her report of the Master's treasures placed in her care, there will be questions and answers like these:

"'Where are the boys and girls I gave thee?'

"'Lord, I was busy keeping my house clean and in order, and my children wandered away.'

"'Where wert thou while thy sons and thy daughters were learning lessons of dishonesty, malice, and impurity?'

"'Lord, I was polishing furniture and making beautiful rugs!'

"'What hast thou to show for thy life-work?'

"'The tidiest house, Lord, and the best starching and ironing in all our neighborhood!'

"Oh, these children! these children! The restless eager boys and girls whom we love more than our lives! Shall we devote our time and strength to that which perishes while the rich garden of our child's soul lies neglected, with foul weeds choking out all worthy and beautiful growths?

"Fleeting, oh mother, are the days of childhood, and speckless windows, snowy linen, the consciousness that everything about the house is faultlessly bright and clean will be poor comfort in that day wherein we shall discover that our poor boy's feet have chosen the path that shall take him out of the way to all eternity."

Grant me my wish, O Lord,
And let my household be
Devoted to Thyself alone,
A nursery for Thee.
—Unknown.

Here is a tribute from Oswald Chambers, writer, preacher, and teacher:

"Our family life in Perth was a very united one; each evening, after the home-lessons were done, was given up to games of various kinds. We found our enjoyment and entertainment in our home; no outside amusements could possibly compare with the fun and happiness to be found there. We never had any desire to be out playing or walking with chums. Father was very strict in our upbringing, and we can thank God, in looking back, for his faithful training of us. . .

"I feel traits in my character I knew not of before, and it causes me to bow in deeper gratitude for that home training which I have now left, for the training and disciplines of life. Oh, what a mighty influence home life has on us! Indeed, we do not know how deep a debt we owe to our mothers and fathers and their training."

HOME

'Tis whispered in the ear of God,
    'Tis murmured through our tears;
'Tis linked with happy childhood days,
    And blessed in riper years.

That hallowed word is ne'er forgot,
    No matter where we roam;
The purest feelings of the heart,
    Still cluster round our home.

Dear resting-place, where weary thought
    May dream away its care,
Love's gentle star unveils her light,
    And shines in beauty there.
        —Fanny J. Crosby.

The Christian home should be the happiest spot on earth, not only to the "grown-ups" but to every member of the family. Let us see that we make it so even to the youngest. Never mind if they do make a noise and tumble the house about with their innocent games, and shout choruses when some of us older ones are trying to write articles in the next room.

Thousands upon thousands of young people have gone to utter destruction for the reason that having cold, dull, stiff firesides at home they sought amusement elsewhere. How many sad parents today would give the world to hear the noisy steps of long-absent children. They would not mind how much the house was turned upside down, nor how dirty the carpets became, if only they could hear once more the cheery voice and feel the clinging arms about their necks and the warm cheeks laid upon theirs! So let us keep them at home by making home the very loveliest place on earth to them, the place of all others where God is honored, and where the whole atmosphere is filled with love and joy and peace.—Reader Harris.

Children are often able to give the most apt of definitions. In the following old ballad we learn what a "home" is as only a child can express it:

> "Some children were playing one day in the street
>   When a poor little girl drew nigh.
> They laughed at her dress and the home she lived in
>   Till the tears slowly came to her eyes.
> One boy roughly said, 'We won't play with you,
>   Because you're too poor, you see.
> Besides, you don't live in a mansion like us.'
>   And the maiden replied tenderly:
> 'It's not the house that makes the home, my mama teaches me.
>   And in our house, a little cot, we're as happy as can be.
> Although we have no mansion grand, bedecked with wealth and pride,
>   Oh, it's not the HOUSE that makes the home,
>   It's the LOVE that is inside.'"

A housing shortage compelled a young doctor, his wife, and three children to live temporarily in a hotel. A sympathetic friend asked the six-year-old daughter of the family if it wasn't too bad that they did not have a home. The child with great surprise replied, "Oh, we have a home, but we just don't have a house to put it in."

Another little girl was once asked where she lived. With a fond look at her mother nearby, she answered spontaneously, "Where Mama is, there's where I live."

When the carpenter has finished your house and hands you the key, that is not your home; it is not yet complete. I remember what happened with my own home, how after it had been furnished came the wife, then one child, and then another, and so by degrees ties were added, and the house grew into a home.—H. W. Beecher.

You can build a house, but a home must grow.—Myrtle Reed.

WHAT MAKES A HOME?

What makes a home? Four walls of polished stone?
   Or brick and mortar laid with nicest care
   Nay! Prison walls are made without as fair.
   Within—look not within—corruption there
   With ignorance and sin defiles the air.

What makes a home? 'Twere better far to roam
   Unhoused than have a part in dainty halls,
   Where purest gems of art adorn the walls,
   If there's no hearth-fire bright for poorest poor
   Who linger in the night without the door.

What makes a home? 'Tis where the weary come
   And lay their burdens down, assured of rest.
   'Tis where we learn to know our dearest best;
   Where little children play, blessing and blest—
   Though walls of coarsest clay enwrap the nest.
                   —Fanny S. Reeder.

The motto, "Christ is the Head of this house," used to be one of the most common adornments on the living-room wall. This simple acknowledgment of Jesus' rightful place in the soul's workshop was a benediction in itself. But in too many of our modern homes, we fear the little motto has been relegated to the dustbin, or to some dusty attic box. While no visual substitute in words has taken its place, our expensive wallpapers, drapes, gadgets, and beautiful china all shout out in chorus: "Money and material things rule this house."

Instead of the well-worn Bible with its words of wisdom and warning about the transitory nature of "things," we have the racks stuffed with the latest magazines on "house improvements" and the latest in house decorations. Make no mistake, the accent cannot be on both the eternal and the temporary; the choice is between a soul's workshop or a showroom and pleasure palace. Our children will grow up to put the emphasis on money, self-indulgence, and soul-marring pleasures, which all make for unhappy future homes and divorce courts. As someone so aptly put it: "'Tis tragic to tie the ship of the soul, in this life, to the pier of things."

The Christ-like graces and their accompanying virtues of courtesy, benevolence, selflessness, thoughtfulness, self-restraint, and gratitude are only to be found where mother and father have fought to keep the home in these modern days, a workshop of the soul.

"It was only after years of study and careful seeking," we are told, "that Leonardo Da Vinci was able to complete his painting of Christ in that lovely picture, 'The Last Supper.' As the great work neared completion, a friend came to see it. Straightway his eye caught sight of the beautiful carved and jeweled chalice that Christ held in His hands. It was a wondrous thing. He complimented the artist on its creation, touching but lightly on the other fine points of the picture.

"Alone in his studio, Da Vinci saw that in the perfection of that lovely chalice he had failed, and hours later, after an inward struggle, he took up his brush and painted it out, replacing it with a simple glass tumbler. By and by the friend returned. Hardly had he entered when he cried, 'What have you done? What have you done with that lovely cup? You have spoiled the picture for me!'

"'I've painted it out,' was the answer. 'I didn't want you to look at the cup; I wanted you to see only Christ.'"

Just so, many parents may have to take up the brush of self-denial and obliterate the chalice of "material gain and self-indulgence," thus putting Christ and the soul in proper perspective for the young onlookers.—E. & L. Harvey.

GOD GIVE US HOMES!

God give us homes!
Homes where the Bible is honored and taught;
Homes with the Spirit of Christ in their thought;
Homes that a likeness to Heaven have caught.
God give us homes!

God give us homes!
Homes with the father in priest-like employ;
Homes that are bright with a far-reaching joy;
Homes where no world-stain shall come to annoy.
God give us homes!

God give us homes!
Homes where the mother is queen-like in love;
Ruled in the fear of the Savior above;
Homes that to youth most inspiring shall prove.
God give us homes!

God give us homes!
Homes with the children to brighten the hours;
Budding and blooming like beautiful flowers;
Places of sunshine—sweet, sanctified bowers.
God give us homes!
—Jno. R. Clements.

Copyright by Lillenas Publishing Co., U.S.A.)

"Now therefore let it please thee to bless the house of thy servant, that it may be before thee for ever: for thou blessest, O Lord, and it shall be blessed for ever" (I Chron. 17:27).

GOD BLESS YOUR HOME

God bless your home
    And all within,
The friends who come;
    Your kith and kin;
Your shelt'ring roof,
    Your homely fare,
Your place of rest,
    Your toil and care.
Bless absent ones
    And those you love,
And guard and guide
    Them from above.
And grant that soon
    Sweet peace will reign
In this and ev'ry land again.
              —Anon.

PRAYER FOR BLESSING

God bless this home—
May all who come within its walls
Good welcome find,
And gain much-needed rest
Of body, soul, and mind.
Let Christ be honored Guest,
His Presence ever rest
In benediction sweet
On all who meet
Here, in this home.

God grant this home be filled with joy
And happy pleasure—let naught destroy
The peace this home shall give,
And may it help each one to live
A little nearer ev'ry day
To Him Who is life's surest stay.
        —Prebendary J. E. S. Harrison.

Could I climb to the highest place in Athens, I would lift my voice and proclaim: "Fellow-citizens, why do ye turn and scrape every stone to gather wealth, and take so little care of your children, to whom one day you must relinquish it all?"—Socrates.

"A child left to himself bringeth his mother to shame"
(Prov. 29:15).

CHAPTER VIII

FULL-TIME OR PART-TIME SCULPTORS?

"A lady was calling upon a friend," relates S. D. Gordon, "whose two children were brought in during the call. As they talked together the caller said eagerly, and yet with evidently no thought of the meaning of her words, 'Oh, I'd give my life to have two such children!'

"And the mother replied with a subdued earnestness whose quiet told of the depth of experience out of which her words came. 'That's exactly what it costs!'"

The minister who told the above story was not the only thinking person who realized the sacrifice of time and effort needed to be given by the parent if the soul of the child were to prosper. We came across this striking statement made by Enid Blyton, the famous children's author, when protesting against the nation's drive for mother-labor in industry during the last war:

"Persuading thousands of young mothers to go out to work and to abandon the care of their children to others is one of the most disastrous things at the present time. What is it going to profit the nation, if we gain the dollars—or even the whole world— but lose the souls of our children? Now that the State is lifting so much responsibility from parents, the bond of love between parents and their children is in danger of being loosened. It is when the mothers of the nation begin to fail in their duty to their children that religion disappears, moral standards fail, and the nation begins to go down."

LOST—A BOY!

Not kidnapped by bandits and hidden in a cave to weep and starve and raise a nation to frenzied searching. Were that the case, one hundred thousand men would rise to the rescue, if need be. Unfortunately, the losing of this lad is without dramatic excitement, though very sad and very real.

The fact is his father lost him. Being too busy to sit with him at the fireside and answer his trivial questions during the years when fathers are the only great heroes of the boys, he let go his hold.

And his mother lost him. Being so much occupied with teas, dinners, and club programs, she let the maid hear the boy say his prayers, and thus her grip slipped, and the boy was lost to his home.

Aye, the Church lost him. Being so occupied with sermons for the wise and elderly who pay the bills, and having good care for dignity, the ministers and elders were unmindful of the human feelings of the boy in the pew, and made no provision in sermon or song or personal contact for his boyishness. And so the Church and many sad-hearted parents are now looking earnestly for the lost boy.—Unknown.

A young man stood at the bar of a court of justice to be sentenced for forgery. The judge had known him from a child, for his father had been a famous legal light and his work on the "Law of Trusts" was the most exhaustive work on the subject in exercise.

"Do you remember your father?" asked the judge sternly, "that father whom you have disgraced?"

The prisoner answered: "I remember him perfectly. When I went to him for advice or companionship, he would look up from his book on the 'Law of Trusts' and say, 'Run away, boy, I'm busy.' My father finished his book, and here I am." The great lawyer had neglected his own trust with awful results.—Talmage.

WHICH MISSION IS MOTHER'S?

She's a woman with a mission;
'Tis her Heaven-born ambition
To reform the world's condition
    You will please to understand.

She's a model of propriety,
A leader of society,
And has a great variety
    Of remedies at hand.

Each a sovereign specific
With a title scientific,
For the cure of things morbific
    That vex the people sore.

For the swift alleviation
Of the evils of the nation
Is her foreordained vocation
    On this sublunary shore.

And while thus she's up and coming,
Always hurrying and humming,
And occasionally slumming,
    This reformer of renown:

Her neglected little Dicky,
Ragged, dirty, tough, and tricky,
With his fingers soiled and sticky,
    Is the terror of the town.
                —*Tit-bits.*

    A distressed father once came to Campbell Morgan asking him how he could regain the confidence and respect of his small son. Can you imagine his surprise at the simplicity of the suggested remedy when Campbell Morgan asked: "Have you ever tried a game of marbles with him?"

TIRED MOTHERS

A little elbow leans upon your knee—
    Your tired knee that has so much to bear;
A child's dear eyes are looking lovingly
    From underneath a thatch of tangled hair.
Perhaps you do not heed the velvet touch
    Of warm, moist fingers holding you so tight;
You do not prize the blessing overmuch—
    You almost are too tired to pray tonight.

But it is blessedness! A year ago
    I did not see it as I do today—

We are all so dull and thankless, and too slow
    To catch the sunshine till it slips away.
And now it seems surpassing strange to me
    That while I wore the badge of motherhood
I did not kiss more oft and tenderly
    The little child that brought me only good.

And if, some night, when you sit down to rest,
    You miss the elbow from your tired knee,
This restless, curly head from off your breast,
    This lisping tongue that chatters constantly;
If from your own the dimpled hands had slipped,
    And ne'er should nestle in your palm again;
If the white feet into the grave had tripped—
    I could not blame you for your heartache then.

I wonder so that mothers ever fret
    At little children clinging to their gowns;
Or that the footprints, when the days are wet,
    Are ever black enough to make them frown!
If I could find a little muddy boot,
    Or cap, or jacket, on my chamber floor—
If I could kiss a rosy, restless foot,
    And hear it patter in my house once more;

If I could mend a broken cart today,
    Tomorrow make a kite to reach the sky—
There is no woman in God's world could say
    She was more blissfully content than I!
But, ah, the dainty pillow next my own
    Is never rumpled by a shining head.
My singing birdling from its nest has flown—
    The little boy I used to kiss—is dead!

                                        —Anon.

    Yes, the greatest regret parents will have when the birdlings have flown will be that they did not spend time with them. Happy the parent who discovers that the most precious thing in his child's estimation is a little of his own time and attention. An ice-cream, or a ticket to a cinema show is poor compensation for the loss of a little attention. The happiest memories of childhood cluster around the times when parents and children worked or played together. Pent-up resentment and a great sense of loss build up in the mind of a child who has no such memories.

One of the happy memories is of a portion of time taken in the evening. Each day to a child is a miniature lifetime. The approach of darkness brings to the mind the sense of the ending of a chapter, and no child truly wants to end it wrongly. A little one that can open its heart on the wrongs or perplexities of the day, will sleep with a sense of well-being, and begin a new day with a better chance of going right, because the sense of guilt has been lost with the childish confession to mother or father the night before. Fear of the dark, or dreaded nightmares many times may be the result of a little heart that has been overloaded with the happenings of the day and has found nowhere to unburden them.—E. & L. Harvey.

THE IDEAL MOTHER

There's something in my mother's eyes when bedtime comes at night
    That makes me want to look at her and do the thing that's right.
At bedtime, mother's eyes are strange, they are so soft and true,
    Her words are very gentle and her hands are gentle too. . . .

I ask her questions when I'm there beside her on the floor,
    That I don't like to ask till then, or never thought before.
Of course her eyes can't talk, I know, but, when I look, I see
    There's something in them every time that must be just for me.
I do not tell her what I see, nor of the pain it brings;
    It is a sort of pain that makes me want to do good things.

—John Martin.

"I take such a proportion of time as I can best spare every night to discourse with each child by itself," writes Susannah Wesley. "On Monday I talk with Molly; on Tuesday with Hetty; Wednesday with Nancy; Thursday with Jacky (John); Friday with Patty; Saturday with

Charles; and with Emilia and Sukey together on Sunday."

Such an effort could not but bear fruit, and it is touching to read a portion of a letter written to her years later by her son, John, who found himself in a time of deep perplexity:

"In many things you have interceded for me and prevailed. Who knows but that in this too you may be successful? If you can spare me only that little part of Thursday evening which you formerly bestowed upon me in another manner, I doubt not it would be as useful now in correcting my heart as it was then for forming my judgment."

THE CHILDREN'S HOUR

> "Between the dark and the daylight,
> When the night is beginning to lower,
> Comes a pause in the day's occupations,
> That is known as the Children's Hour."

When Longfellow wrote his beautiful poem there was a Children's Hour in almost every home. How many busy mothers of today spend with their children those most sacred moments, the bedtime hour?

"Please tell me a story, Mother." This is the universal plea of childhood, especially at bedtime. Many a mother is puzzled as to how to respond.

Too often the busy mother says, "I cannot tell you a story." To an older child she may add, "Run away and read your own story."

She does not realize that she is building an invisible barrier between herself and her child. When the child has been told this repeatedly he does read his own story, and he does not ask mother's advice in regard to the selection.

A love for good literature begins in the nursery with the stories mother tells. Later, the child will learn to choose for himself th best books and will enjoy reading them aloud with mother.—Anon.

WHICH MOTHER ARE YOU?

A woman sat by a hearthside place
Reading a book, with a pleasant face,
Till a child came up, with a childish frown,
And pushed the book saying, "Put it down."
Then the mother, slapping his curly head,
Said, "Troublesome child, go off to bed;
A great deal of Christ's life I must know
To train you up as a child should go."
And the child went off to bed to cry,
And renounce religion—by and by.

Another woman bent over a book
With a smile of joy and an intent look,
Till a child came up and jogged her knee,
And said of the book, "Put it down—take me."
Then the mother sighed as she stroked his head,
Saying softly, "I never shall get it read;
But I'll try by loving to learn His will,
And His love into my child instill."
That child went to bed without a sigh,
And will love religion—by and by.
—Selected.

The care of children demands time and effort. There are many attractions for young couples outside their homes, and it is easy to fall victim to the temptation to leave the children to themselves, or to others, because of the time and trouble and the loss of social pleasures. Within the welfare state, the development of social agencies hitherto has taken place for the most part outside the home, but, quite apart from this, many observers think that there has been in the last fifty years a decline in the strength of the family itself as an institution.—Rt. Hon. Gwilym Lloyd-George, in a speech at Northampton at the Free Church Federal Council.

The most memorable scene in my childhood was father and mother at morning and evening prayers. Your son may go to the ends of the earth, and run through the whole catalogue of transgressions, but he will remember the family altar, and it will be a check, and a call, and perhaps his redemption.—Talmage.

All successful parents have had a pause in the day's occupations where, together, they read the Master Sculptor's directions, promises, warnings, and counsels contained in the Good Book—the Bible.
—E. & L. Harvey.

"From a child thou hast known the holy scriptures"
(II Tim. 3:15).

"The unfeigned faith that is in thee . . . dwelt first in thy grandmother Lois, and thy mother Eunice; and I am persuaded that in thee also" (II Tim. 1:5).

CHAPTER IX

THE FAMILY STUDIES THE MASTER SCULPTOR'S PLANS

A little fellow was exploring the cupboard under the stairs. One thing after another met his curious eyes, when finally he spied a dust-covered Bible.

"Mummy, is this God's Book?" he asked.

"Yes, dear," she answered.

"Then why don't we send it back to Him? We never use it."

"We never use it," could be said of the Bible in many of the homes of today. In this modern age of ours with advanced educational and living standards, we are prone to disparage all the old-fashioned ways. In fact, the way to scare someone nowadays is to cynically say—"Oh, they did that fifty or one hundred years ago."

Someone has said, "A family that prays together, stays together."

—E. F. & L. Harvey.

WHEN FATHER READS THE BOOK

In these days of rush and bustle
  When we hurry off to work,
I'm reminded of those early times
  When father read the Book.
When father read the Book,
  As we each our places took
Round the dear old family altar
  While father read the Book.

O those dear old Bible stories,
  Psalms that flowed like rippling brook;
Warnings, promises, and precepts
  Lived, as father read that Book.
As father read the Book,
  Satan's kingdom round us shook,
And our Savior early claimed us
  Because father read the Book.

> O they say it was old-fashioned,
>   And what waste of time 'twould look
> To now take half-an-hour
>   To let father read the Book.
>   But as father read the Book,
>   Blessed thoughts in our minds stuck;
> And the day went so much better
>   Just 'cause father read the Book.
>
> Oft I'm troubled as I journey
>   On toward Heav'n with upward look,
> To see families all about me
>   Grow up without father's Book.
>   Let father read the Book,
>   Kneel and pray and read the Book;
> Your home will be so different
>   If your father reads the Book.
>   —H. E. Foster.

Dr. Charles A. Blanchard in his book, *Getting Things From God*, tells this striking story:

"It is said that a little girl in a worldly home was permitted at one time to visit her grandfather. This was an old-fashioned Christian home, where each day there was a time to pray, to read the Bible, to sing Christian hymns.

"After a few weeks her mother came to take her home. The little thing objected. She wished to stay at her grandfather's. Her mother was mortified and somewhat nettled. She said to the little child, 'Do you not wish to go home with your mother?'

"And the child replied, 'Yes, Mamma, I would like to go home with you, but you know there is not any God at our house. Grandpa has a God at his home and I like to stay where there is a God.'"

J. Edgar Hoover, once chief of the F.B.I., said: "If there is any hope for the future of America, if there is to be peace and happiness in our homes, then we, as a nation, must return to God and the practice of daily prayer. Can we have eternal peace without morality? Can we build homes without God, or have worthy parents who do not know and practice His teachings? Our nation is sadly in need of rebirth of the simple life—a return to the days when God was a part of each household, when families arose in the morning with a prayer on their lips and ended the day by gathering together to place themselves in His care.

"A godless home is built upon sands; it is an inviting breeding ground for moral decay and crime. My hope for the future of this nation is predicated upon the faith of God, which is nurtured in the family."

We recently read of a famous playwright and novelist, who, feeling his powers were failing him, became greatly depressed. Just a few days before he committed suicide, he expressed his longing for some form of religion. Some mother and father had failed to give an anchor to the soul when the storms of life beat upon him.

Charles Kingsley once wrote a letter to a famous scientist and agnostic, endeavoring to comfort him upon the loss of a son, with thoughts on the resurrection. The scientist replied in these words:

"I neither deny nor affirm the immortality of man. I see no reason for believing in it, but, on the other hand, I have no means of disproving it ... Kicked into the world, a boy without guide or training, or with worse than none, I confess to my shame that few men have drunk deeper of all kinds of sin than I. Happily, my course was arrested in time—before I had earned absolute destruction—and for long years I have been slowly and painfully climbing, with many a fall, towards better things."

A chaplain of a U. S. penitentiary once studied the backgrounds of seventeen-hundred of its inmates. "Out of the seventeen-hundred convicts," he said, "I found only one who had been brought up in a home where they had had an old-fashioned family altar. I have heard since that he was pardoned as he was found innocent of the crime with which he was charged.

"There was an atmosphere in the old-fashioned home, a kind of prophylaxis which made it impossible for skepticism or atheism to live there. May God give us back the old-fashioned Bible, and old-fashioned parents, and then the Holy Spirit will come down on your little home like the glory cloud came down and went into the Tabernacle."

Two young men faced the death sentence for murdering a gas station attendant during a robbery. With the last hours of their lives slowly ebbing away, they jointly penned this pathetic statement:

"We wish to say, in partial excuse for ourselves, that we did not have a fair chance in life. Coming from broken homes, we grew up in neglect. In youth we were denied parental care, affection, and guidance.

"Religious training would have pointed us in the right direction, but we were not taken to Sunday School or to church services. While in prison during the long years of waiting, we have tried to build up in our souls what was lacking . . . May our tragic lives and ending serve as a warning to all—young and old."

> God, God, may every household take to heart
> The old earth's desperate need and rear its altars
> Close by its own hearthside—and peace, long sought,
> Will lave the earth because of mankind's heeding
> The vital lessons that the Master taught.
> —Grace Noll Crowell.

There is one mark of the household in which God is known and loved, which is too often wanting in our day; I mean the practice of family prayer. Depend upon it, the worth of every practice of the kind can only be measured by its effect during a long period of time. Family prayers, though occupying only a few minutes, do make a great difference to any household at the end of a year.
—Canon Liddon.

A house without a roof would be scarcely less a home than a family unsheltered by God's friendship.—Horace Bushnell.

An evangelist, after much experience in the inquiry room, said:
"I do not know anything that has encouraged me more in laboring for children than my experience in the inquiry room. In working there, I have found out that those who had religious training, whose parents strove early to lead them to Christ, have been the easiest to lead toward Him. I always feel as though I have a lever to work with when I know that a man has been taught by a godly father and mother; even though his parents died when he was young, the impression that they died praying for him has always a great effect through life."

FAMILY ALTAR FRAGRANCE

How far the holy fragrance of
    The family altar goes;
When childhood days are far behind
    The beauty of it glows.

Though some things, to my memory,
    Are indistinct and blurred,
I still can hear my father's voice
    Expound the Holy Word.

I did not heed its counsel then,
    Or realize its worth;
But now I know that shrine to be
    The sweetest place on earth.

It's proved a shield to keep my faith
    Undimmed through joy and care;
The mem'ry of that hallowed place—
    My father's voice in prayer.
              —Unknown.

We cannot conclude without presenting the convincing array of tributes to the "family altar." We trust these will prove an incentive to rebuild this sacred institution.

God wants time with us alone to tell us secrets for the sake of our children. Oh, the inexpressible and lasting blessing of having a father and mother who were familiar with God, a man and a woman to whom He whispered, told His secrets, and who lived out in their own lives the grace and glory born of such communion. Let us be very careful lest by our neglect of hospitality to God and of listening to His confidences, our children miss the way. For the sake of the children, God told Abraham His secrets.—G. Campbell Morgan.

The venerated Rev. Philip Henry, the father of Matthew Henry the commentator, was a very godly man. In his biography it is said, "He and his wife constantly prayed together, morning and evening."

We are told, also, that he made a conscience of family worship and abounded in it. He said to his children and friends, "Be sure you look to your secret duty; keep that up, whatever you do; the soul cannot prosper in the neglect of it. Apostasy generally begins at the closet door. . . . If the worship of God be not in the home, write, 'Lord, have mercy on us' on the door, for there is a plague, a curse in it."

Praying Hyde, the missionary to India who left such a fragrant memory of his soul-winning efforts and prayer-life, owed much to the family altar where his father repeatedly asked that God would thrust out laborers into His great harvest field. It was no wonder that God should call his two sons into the ministry, and one of his daughters into active, Christian work.

The home of Hudson Taylor, founder of the China Inland Mission, was a model to follow in every way, but especially when it came to the family altar. His biographer has this to say:

"The spiritual life of his children was equally with the mother, the father's care. Family worship he conducted regularly, after both breakfast and tea. Every member of the household had to be present, and the passage read was explained in such practical fashion that even the children could not fail to see its application. He was very particular about giving them the whole Word of God, omitting nothing. The Old Testament as well as the New was taken in regular course . . .

"On Sundays he gave even more time to this home-ministry, in spite of the services for which he was responsible, and that often involved a considerable journey on foot. While thoroughly approving of Sunday Schools for those who needed them, he did not consider his own children to be among the number, and would relinquish to no one the privilege of teaching them in the things of God."

Joseph Parker's biographer says: "From his earliest days the boy was the subject of religious influences. The Bible was the book most read in his father's house, and thus from infancy, the future preacher was nurtured on the Word of God."

MY FIRST ALTAR

I have knelt at altars of marble and gold,
Or of costly wood, far-famed and old,
   And hallowed by stained-glass ray;
But ever my memory leaps the years
To that altar of childhood's hopes and tears—
   My mother's knee . . . The day,

However full of joy or woe,
Brought us at eve, a white-robed row,
   To my mother's knee for prayer.
"Now I lay me"—with faces pressed
To her comforting lap, her tender breast,
   We plead our Father's care.

The altar cloth, her apron white,
Where wee hands clung in baby plight—
   Her badge of service this.

> The crooning hymn . . . the story hour . . .
> Our sermon, rich in love and power . . .
>   The benediction kiss.
>
> So I close my eyes to the marble and gold
> And kneel again as in years of old
>   At that shrine in the heart of me;
> And the childish words say themselves, in part,
> For at prayer I am ever a child at heart,
>   At the altar of mother's knee.
>   —Unknown.

Often, when fathers, for whatever reason, were not available to lead in family prayers, mothers have been left with the task of reading the Scriptures to the children.

Booth-Tucker, the biographer of Mrs. Catherine Booth, the mother of the Salvation Army, writes thus of her early childhood:

"Especially was she (Mrs. Mumford, the mother) anxious to encourage her daughter in the study of the Book which she looked upon as the supreme fountain of wisdom. It was from the Bible that Catherine received her earliest lessons. Many a time would she stand on a footstool at her mother's side, when but a child of five, reading to her from its pages. Before she was twelve years old she had read the sacred Book from cover to cover eight times through, thus laying the foundation of that intimate knowledge and exceptional familiarity with the divine revelation which made so profound an impression upon all who knew her."

Another striking illustration of a mother's influence is seen in the early history of Philip Doddridge, whose name is ever associated with *The Family Expositor* and *The Rise and Progress of Religion in the Soul*. He first saw the light in an obscure street in London, a frail flower then, for he was laid away soon after birth as dead. He had a mother of earnest prayer and living piety. She taught her children to love the Scriptures, by describing the scenes in the Bible, in a familiar manner, on the old Dutch tiles which lined the chimney corner. Little did the mother of Doddridge anticipate his future career, when he reclined on her knee, followed the direction of her fingers in the Bible, and in childlike simplicity listened to the words of eternal life. When she laid her hand on his head and prayed that he might be a child of God, she did not know that God was preparing him, through her instrumentality, to stand up in the pulpit at Northampton, on Castle Hill, and preach the Gospel with so much success.—Anon.

Whatever merit there is in anything that I have written, is simply due to the fact that, when I was a child, my mother daily read me a part of the Bible and daily made me learn a part of it by heart.
—John Ruskin.

The mother of Phillips Brooks always told Bible stories to her boys after they were in bed. Who may compute the influences communicated in this manner to the great preacher who was destined to become so potent a factor in the world of thought?—Anon.

"How often have I blessed the memory of those divine passages of experimental divinity which I have heard from her mouth," said Bishop Hall, speaking of his mother.

Adam Clarke, the commentator, said: "For my mother's religious teachings, I shall have endless reasons to bless my Maker."

Before the Communists overran China, Madame Chiang Kai-Shek was a prominent figure in the political world. She attributed much of her influence in China to her mother's godly upbringing:
"I knew my mother lived very close to God. I recognized something great in her. And I believe that my childhood training influenced me greatly, even though I was more or less rebellious at the time. It must often have grieved my beloved mother that I found family prayers tiresome and frequently found myself conveniently thirsty at the moment, so that I had to slip out of the room. Like my

brothers and sisters, I always had to go to church, and I hated the long sermons. But today I feel that this churchgoing habit established something, a kind of stability, for which I am grateful to my parents.

"My mother was not a sentimental parent. In many ways she was Spartan. But one of my strongest childhood impressions is of mother going to a room she kept for the purpose on the third floor to pray. She spent hours in prayer, often beginning before dawn. When we asked her advice about anything, she would say, 'I must ask God first.' And we could not hurry her. Asking God was not a matter of spending five minutes to ask Him to bless her child and grant the request. It meant waiting upon God until she felt His leading. And I must say that whenever Mother prayed and trusted God for her decision, the undertaking invariably turned out well."

FIRESIDE MEMORIES

An old-time hymn—
And in my heart is stirred
Memories dearer to me than all the world:
Father, Mother, in the soft firelight
Singing, singing in pure delight
That hymn of love and praise.
Our childish voices sweet and shrill
Blending with theirs;
And then a hush as Father prays
That God will keep us all our days.

And then with bated breath
We listen while he tells
Of Daniel in the lions' den,
And three men in the fiery furnace;
And then, as plain as day we see
Christ walking on the sea of Galilee.
'Most every hymn we know,
And mother's face, how sweet it is,
There in the firelight glow.

> O, children of the present day,
> Who do not know
> The joy of family worship
> Within the firelight glow,
> I would not trade these memories
> For all that you might give!
> What can you know of worship?
> Who'll teach you how to live?
> The mothers are too busy,
> The fathers do not pray;
> Oh, in my heart I pity you,
> Ye children of today.
> —Alice Baker.

The absurdity of neglecting the culture of the soul is shown by an incident in the life of Coleridge:

"An English deist, calling upon Coleridge, inveighed bitterly against the rigid instruction in Christian homes. 'Consider,' said he, 'the helplessness of a little child. Before it has wisdom or judgment to decide for itself, it is prejudiced in favor of Christianity. How selfish is the parent who stamps the hot iron with his model. I shall prejudice my children, neither for Christianity nor for Buddhism nor for atheism, but allow them to wait for their mature years. Then they can open the question and decide for themselves.'

"Later the poet led his atheist acquaintance into the garden. Suddenly he exclaimed: 'How selfish is the gardener who ruthlessly stamps his prejudice in favor of roses, and violets, and strawberries into a receptive garden bed! The time was when in April I pulled up the young weeds, the parsley, and thistle, and planted the garden beds out with vegetables and flowers. Now, I have decided to permit the garden to go until September. Then the black clods can choose for themselves between cockleberries and currants and strawberries.'"

Educate children without religion, and you make a race of clever devils.—Willington.

"How shall we order the child, and how shall we do unto him?"
(Judges 13:12).

A partnership with God is parenthood.
What strength, what purity, what self-control,
What love, what wisdom should belong to them,
Who help God fashion an immortal soul!
—Unknown.

CHAPTER X

THE CHISELING

(THE TRAINING OF THE CHILD)

This is a chapter about good hard work! The welcoming of the child is a joy; the vision of what he may become is uplifting, but the chiseling daily on the character demands patient, arduous toil. Henry Ward Beecher gives us an excellent definition of child-training:

"'Train up a child in the way he should go, and when he is old he will not depart from it.' It does not say, 'Educate the child,' but 'Train up the child.' To educate a man is to tell him what to do, while to train him is to see that he does it. Training is the rubbing of education into muscle and bone. If you tell a child what is good, it does not follow that he will not depart from it, but if you train him into being good, he will not depart from it. If you tell him that he must be orderly, he may not be, but if you see that he is orderly till he is grown up, he cannot get rid of the habit of being so. If you tell him that he must not lie, that he must speak the truth, it is not certain that he will obey, but if you see that he forms a habit of being ashamed of lying, the habit of speaking the truth will be so wrought into his mind that he will never depart from it. Habits formed in childhood are faster than colors dyed in the wool."

Catherine Booth defines child-training in this way:
"Let us look at the word 'train.' It does not merely mean to teach. Mother, if you want to train your child you must practice what you teach, and you must show him how to practice it also, and you must, at all costs of trouble and care, see that he does it.
"Suppose, by way of illustration, that you have a vine, and that this vine is endowed with reason, and will, and moral sense. You say to your vine-dresser: 'Now, I want that vine trained,' that is, made to grow in a particular way, so that it may bear the largest amount of

fruit possible to it. Suppose your vine-dresser goes to your vine every morning, and says to it, 'Now, you must let that branch grow in this direction, and that branch grow in another; you are not to put forth too many shoots here, nor too many tendrils there.' Having told it what to do and how to grow, he shuts it up and leaves it to itself.

"This is precisely the way many good people act towards their children. But lo, the vine grows as it likes! Nature is too strong for mere theory; words will not curb its exuberance, nor check its waywardness. Your vine-dresser must do something more effectual than talking. He must nail that branch where he wishes it to grow; he must cut away what he sees to be superfluous; he must lop and prune and dress it, if it is to be trained for beauty and for fruitfulness.

"And just so, mother, if you want your child to be trained for God and righteousness, you must prune, and curb, and propel, and lead it in the way in which it should go. But some mother says, 'What a deal of trouble!' Ah, that is just why many parents fail; they are afraid of trouble, but if you will not take the trouble to train Charlie when he is a little boy, he will give you a great deal more trouble when he is a big one."

SOUL CULTURE

I said unto my gardener,
    "I want my vine to bear
The choicest, richest, largest grapes
    To be seen anywhere."
So he tied it here
And he cut it there,
    And he trained it along the wall,
And oh! the loveliest grapes appeared—
    The wonder of us all.

God said unto the mother,
    "I want your child to be
A godly, helpful, useful man—
    A messenger for Me."

> So she curbed him here,
> And she taught him there,
> > And she urged him to what was right,
> > And o'er the heads of ill-trained sons,
> > He towered in moral height.
> > > —H. E. Foster.

Training a child is the highest and holiest and most fascinating of all occupations. And it takes the most heart power and brain power combined of any, too. The way to train the child is to train yourself. What you are, he will be. If your hands are morally dirty, his life will be dirtied by the home-handling he gets.—S. D. Gordon.

> If you would bind your little one to you,
> Bind your own soul to all that is high and true,
> And let its light shine clear through all you do.
> > —Frobel.

It is not possible to teach a child what you do not believe. While your tongue says one thing and your mind clings to another, the child hears your mind and follows its thought, always.

Teaching is not a matter of routined words at all. It is a communication between two minds, unspoken, unseen, but felt with unmistakable clarity.

You cannot hide doubt, or anger, or love. You can hide no thought of your mind from the listening, watchful child beside you. He may not be able to put it into words; you may not have the power to do so, either. You feel, and he feels your feeling, and the communication has been made.

That is why you cannot teach religion to a child unless you possess it in your mind and soul and practice it while you live out your days before him.—Unknown.

> Mother! Mother! Watch and pray!
> Fling not golden hours away!
> > Now or never, plant and sow,
> > Catch the morning's earliest glow.

Mother! Mother! Guard the dew,
While it sparkles clear and true!
    No delay! The scorching noon
    May thy treasures reach too soon.

Mother! Point them to the sky;
Tell them of a loving eye,
    That more tender is than thine,
    And doth ever on them shine.

Mother! Lead them soon and late
To behold the golden gate;
    When they long to enter there,
    Lead them to the Lamb by prayer.

Mother! Seize the precious hours,
While the dew is on thy flowers!
    Life is such a fleeting thing;
    Mother! Mother! Sow in Spring!
        —Selected.

When once china or porcelain has been inscribed, and put into a furnace, and baked and glazed, you cannot rub the inscription off. It is too late then. If you want to rub it off, you must do it while the ware is in the "biscuit." When children come into our hands they are in the "biscuit," and we can inscribe on them what we please.

—H. W. Beecher.

MOLDING

I took a piece of common clay,
And idly fashioned it one day;
And as my fingers pressed it still,
It moved and yielded at my will.
I came again when days were past,
The bit of clay was hard at last;
The form I gave it still it bore,
But I could change that form no more.

> I took a piece of living clay,
> And gently formed it day by day,
> And molded with my power and art
> A young child's soft and yielded heart.
> I came again when days were gone;
> It was a man I looked upon.
> He still that early impress bore,
> And I could change it nevermore.
> —Selected.

When a child is born it feeds on the mother. All that necessary economy which goes before the child's experience resides in the mother. When the child is so grown that its mind begins to be hungry, it eats the mother's mind, just as before it ate the mother's milk. It is dependent on the mother's thought for its own thinking. It has all the apparatus for thinking, but no thoughts of its own. It is a little questioner, asking, "What is that?" and "Who is that?" and "Why is that?" and "Where is that?"—gathering knowledge from the mother's knowledge. The mother precedes and prepares; the child comes after and devours.—H. W. Beecher.

> And say to mothers what a holy charge
> Is theirs—with what a kingly power their love
> Might rule the fountains of the newborn mind.
> Warn them to wake at early dawn, and sow
> Good seed before the world has sown its tares.
> —Mrs. Sigourney.

The picture-book is the child's first educator, and it educates either for good or ill. It educates for ill when pictures of badness are beautifully painted. That becomes an imagination of the heart. Evil is made attractive, fair, heroic—an object to be sought for, a thing to be desired.

Ye who train the young—parents and teachers—beware of the first gallery in which you put the child! Beware of the earliest pictures which its heart will hold! They are the germ-cells of the spirit —they will make or mar. Beware how you suffer a bright color to light upon a vicious form. The vice will grow dim to the eye, but the bright color will remain.

There is only one picture that the child's heart can safely hold: it is the form of Jesus. Put it there early before all things! Let it be the first painting in the soul—the child's first ideal of greatness! Let the morning message of heroism be a message of unselfishness. Not on Caesar, not on Alexander, not on Napoleon, let the opening eye be centered; point it to Jesus! Let it gaze on the glory of what man calls weak, unfit for survival! Let it see the strength of gentleness, the courage of meekness, the might of restraint, the victory of forgiveness, the majesty of patience, the triumph of peacemaking, the manliness of compassion, the Divineness of sacrifice! Let it behold the splendor of that epitaph, "Himself He cannot save," the luster of that inscription, "Obedient unto death"! Let it mark the heroism of that bloodiest of battlefields where love stood dauntless to receive its mortal wound! Let it catch the light of the Dolorous Way, the sheen of Gethsemane, the glow of Calvary—till the heart of the child shall cry, "When I grow up, I will be a Christ!" Then will the tempter vanish, then will the kingdom come, for the victory is already complete when we have imaged the beauty of holiness.—G. Matheson.

It is no kindness at all to shield a child from hard work; we incapacitate them for life when we allow them to shirk their duty. Many a parent has been heard to say: "Oh, childhood comes only once. I slaved hard when young and I want my child to enjoy life." But this father's advice to his son is more wholesome:

"Remember, my son, you have to work. Whether you handle a pick or a pen, a wheelbarrow or a set of books, digging ditches or editing a paper, ringing an auction bell or writing funny things, you must work. If you look around, you will see the men who are most able to live the rest of their days without work are the men who work the hardest.

"Do not be afraid of killing yourself with overwork. It is beyond your power to do that on the sunny side of thirty. They die sometimes, but it is because they quit at 6 a.m. and don't get home until 2 a.m.

"It is the interval that kills, my son. The work gives you an appetite for your meals; it lends solidity to your slumbers; it gives you a perfect and grateful appreciation of rest.

"There are young men who do not work, but the world is not proud of them. It does not know their names even. It simply speaks of them as 'old So-and-so's boys.' Nobody likes them. The great, busy world does not know that they are there.

"So find out what you want to be and do—and take off your coat and make a dust in the world. The busier you are, the less harm you will be apt to get into, the sweeter will be your sleep, the brighter and happier your hours off, and the better satisfied will be the world with you."—Robert Burdette.

YOUR DUTY

When little children try to shirk
From doing any honest work
And always have a good excuse
If asked to be of any use,
They'll find the lazy habit grow
As nearly all the elders know,
And very likely hard to break
Though one may lots of trouble take.
So, start today, and do your bit.
I'm sure you will be glad of it.
—Fanny Allen.

The influence of the well-ordered, sunny-tempered Christian home is incalculable. John Ruskin, in counting up the blessings of his childhood, reckoned these three for first good: Peace—he had never heard father's or mother's voice once raised in any dispute. Next to this he estimated Obedience—he obeyed a word or lifted finger of father or mother as a ship her helm, without any idea of resistance. And, lastly, Faith—nothing was ever promised him that

was not given, nothing ever threatened him that was not inflicted, and nothing ever told him that was not true. It was not strange that such home training went to the making of a great character."
—*The Watchman.*

Keep your word with your child as you would with your banker.
—*My Old Scrapbook.*

Some people tell lies to children with the view of enjoying a laugh at their credulity. This is to make a mock of sin; they are fools who do it. The tendency in a child to believe what is told, is of God for good. It is lovely. It seems a shadow of primeval innocence glancing by. We should reverence a child's simplicity. Touch it only with truth. Be not the first to quench that lovely trustfulness by lies.
—Arnot.

Someone has said, "A loveless discipline provokes children to rebellion. Affection without discipline makes spoiled brats."

A minister once said to his old mother, "Ma, I think you ruled us with too rigid a rod in our boyhood. It would have been better had you used gentler methods." The old lady straightened up and said, "Well, William, when you have raised up three as good preachers as I have, then you can talk."

J. Edgar Hoover, once head of the F.B.I., observed how ridiculous is the modern idea of letting the child decide religious questions for himself:

"Shall I make my child go to Sunday School and church? Yes, and with no further discussion about the matter! Startled? Why? How do you answer Junior when he comes to breakfast on Monday morning and announces to you that he is not going to school any more? You know! Junior goes. How do you answer when Junior comes in very much besmudged and says, 'I'm not going to take a bath'? Junior bathes, doesn't he?

"Why all this timidity then, in the realm of his spiritual guidance and growth? Going to let him wait and decide what church he'll go to when he's old enough? . . . You didn't wait until you were old enough. You don't wait until he's old enough to decide whether or not he wants to go to school—to start an education. You don't wait until he's old enough to decide whether he wishes to be clean or dirty, do you? Do you wait until he's old enough to decide if he wants to take his medicine when he is sick? Do you?

"What shall we say when Junior announces he doesn't like to go to Sunday School and church? That's an easy one to answer. Just be consistent. Tell him, 'Junior, in our house we all go to church and Sunday School, and that includes you.'"

Dr. Dwight thus speaks of the importance of early training:
"The great truths of religion should be taught so early, that the mind should never remember when it began to learn, or when it was without this knowledge. Whenever it turns a retrospective view upon the preceding periods of its existence, these truths should always seem to have been in its possession: to have the character of innate principles, to have been inwoven in its nature, and to constitute a part of all its current thinking."

We parents clothe our children in both senses of the word. We provide the raiment for their bodies, and in no small degree, we provide the habits of their thought and conduct. We make for them coats that will last—which no moth can eat or time deface—coats which they may never outgrow as long as life endures. Mothers! The Creator puts into your hands an unclothed spirit as well as an unclothed body. You make a garment for the one, and in many a home there is hardly a rest for your busy needles through all the year.

"But shall the mind—the immortal spirit—be left naked, or be compelled to pick up at random its habits of thinking and acting? This were impossible. Our children will put on our ways and our habits in spite of us. Our character streams into our children, entering through their eyes and ears, and every faculty of observation.

What they see us do, they will do; what they hear from us lodges in their memory, and, like seeds dropped from a parent stock, will come up in their conduct, for good or evil.—T. Cuyler.

After reading these tributes, it seems absurd to even consider the idea so current among us that children ought not to be taught religion for fear of having their minds biased to some particular creed, but they should be left to themselves till they are capable of making their own choice. We cannot without great impunity overlook God's command on this subject:

"And these words, which I command thee this day, shall be in thine heart: And thou shalt teach them diligently unto thy children, and shalt talk of them when thou sittest in thine house, and when thou walkest by the way, and when thou liest down, and when thou risest up" (Deut. 6:6,7).

We leave no other part of the child's culture to his own choice:

1. We train the manners, lest his lack of courtesy and etiquette be a reflection on his home training. What mother thinks it unfair to take great pains in insisting on her child saying "please" and "thank you"?

2. We train the mind that the child might have the best chance in a competitive world. How absurd it would be to leave to his choice whether or not he went to school! If parents fail here, the School Board steps in.

3. We carefully train the child in habits of health and hygiene. We do not tolerate a dirty face and neck, or unbrushed teeth.

Surely then, if the soul of a child is immortal, it is imperative that we leave nothing to chance.—E. & L. Harvey.

We will not influence our children in making choices and decisions in matters of religion.

Why not?
The advertisements will! The press will!
The radio will! The movies will! (The television will!)
Their neighbors will! Their business will! Their politicians will! We use our influence over flowers, vegetables, cattle. Shall we ignore our children?"—*The Trumpeter.*

How better end this chapter than to present this prayer for parents worded by the godly Andrew Murray:

"O my God! With fear and trembling would I bow before Thee, the righteous God. Impress deeply upon my heart, O Lord, the solemn lessons Thou dost teach Thy Church by the terrible sight of Thy judgment on the house of Eli, Thy servant.

"Not to rule and restrain our children, to give them their own way, is to honor them more than Thee. Ere we think it, weakness becomes wickedness, in ourselves and our children too. Thou hast made every parent after Thine image, a king in his home, that he may rule his home well, and command his children in the way of the Lord. On his exercise of authority, and their rendering of obedience, Thou hast made Thy blessing dependent.

"O God, have mercy upon us. Let the thought of Thy command rule our home. Let Thy judgment on disobedience, Thy promised grace to those who give themselves to obey, Thy blessing on a home ordered in Thy fear, stir us with our whole heart to fulfil our holy calling in Thy fear. And let us, above all, believe that as we and our children in this fulfil Thy will, we are in the path of true blessing for this life and the life to come. Amen."

When God lacks mothers,
His other sculptors
    Patiently chisel each day:
Teachers and preachers
And Sunday School teachers—
    These all form a noble array.
            —Pauline Jessen.

CHAPTER XI

OTHER SCULPTORS

The Sunday School teacher just could not help liking young Johnny, in spite of all his mischief. "And what are you going to be when you get big?" he asked the boy.

"I don't know; depends who gets me. If it's the devil, I may be a gangster; if God gets me, perhaps I'll be a missionary," was the thoughtful reply.

When we think of the thousands of homes where Christ is never named, we wonder who will get the modern Johnny. God has always had a noble army of "other sculptors" who have stepped into the gap made by a parent's death, desertion, or sheer lack of vision.

Worth mentioning, too, are those "supplementary" sculptors who help shape the child during those hours away from home — at school, Sunday School, or in Youth Organizations. Such men or women, often sacrificing a home of their own, and in many cases a life-partner, devote all the love of a deeply affectionate nature to fathering and mothering the coming generation.

Were it possible to assemble those who are fostering, nursing, or teaching the mentally deficient children, the orphans, the undernourished and underprivileged children of our great cities, the leprous and the temple children of heathen lands, then we would have some of the most splendid men and women on earth. Many of these are unknown to the public by name, but their labors are duly recorded by God above, and their work will be enshrined in generous deeds accomplished in the men and women of tomorrow.

—E. & L. Harvey.

> God's first great thought was that parents
> Would teach His way to youth;
> But should they fail, His design prevails—
> He bids others expound His truth.

A faithful nanny or servant girl
    Has oft performed His will,
And on the life of the untaught child
    Has carved His image with skill.

A Müller, Barnardo, or Quarrier
    Has fathered the orphan-child,
And painstakingly sought with utmost care
    His feet on Christ's path to guide.

A teacher at school has daily prayed
    That her hand might help to lead
Those, who at home never heard of Him,
    And thus meet a deep-felt need.

An obscure teacher in Sunday School
    Oft deems he labors in vain;
But the Juvenile Courts who deal with crime
    Appraise such work as "gain."

And daily the Master-Sculptor's plan
    Love's volunteers fulfil.
But with outstretched hands, youth's Christless hordes
    Plead for such sculptors still.
        —Pauline Jessen.

Many, many women, hearing a divine call, have left home and loved ones, and gone out to foreign lands where their lives have been spent in blessing children of other races. Weary hours of teaching and mothering have been unnoticed by the public eye, but they have laid foundations for the coming generations to build upon. Mary Warburton Booth who gave herself to helping little Indian girls, was one of these. Another was Amy Carmichael who dared much in order to rescue the doomed and suffering temple girls. The longing expressed in her poem is equal to any mother's heart-cry:

"Father, hear us, we are praying,
Hear the words our hearts are saying;
We are praying for our children.

"Keep them from the powers of evil,
From the secret, hidden peril;
Father, hear us for our children.

"From the whirlpool that would suck them,
From the treacherous quicksand, pluck them;
Father, hear us for our children.

"From the worldling's hollow gladness,
From the sting of faithless sadness;
Father, Father, keep our children.

"Through life's troubled waters steer them,
Through life's bitter battle cheer them;
Father, Father, be Thou near them.

"Read the language of our longing,
Read the wordless pleadings thronging,
Holy Father, for our children.

"And wherever they may 'bide,
Lead them Home at eventide."
—Amy Carmichael.

Franke, Müller, Quarrier, and Barnardo were men who took the father's place in the lives of thousands of orphans. Though possessing families of their own, God so enlarged their hearts as to make them the soul-sculptors of a multitude of children, robbed of the natural care of parents of their own.

Teachers of boys, such as Dean Farrar, Arnold of Rugby, and many others, have helped to shape at a most critical time the lives of some of the best men of their times. Boys who had come from wealthy homes yet devoid of spiritual training, were on the road to lives of infidelity and profligacy, but were stayed by the prayers, personal entreaties, sermons, and daily influence of such godly men as these. These men were truly soul-sculptors, or to use another picture—bridge-builders.

THE BRIDGE-BUILDER

A traveler going a lone highway,
Came at evening, cold and grey,
To a chasm vast and deep and wide;
The old man passed in the twilight dim,
The sullen stream had no fears for him,
But he paused when safe on the other side,
And built a bridge to span the tide.

"Old man," said a fellow-traveler near,
"You are wasting your strength with building here;
Your journey will end with the ending day,
You never again will pass this way.
You've crossed the chasm deep and wide;
Why build you a bridge on the other side?"

The builder lifted his old, grey head;
"In the path that I have come," he said,
"There followed after me a youth
Whose steps must pass this way forsooth;
The chasm that has been as nought to me,
To that fair-haired youth may a pitfall be.
He, too, must cross in the twilight dim;
My friend, I am building the bridge for him."
—Unknown.

Martin Luther in a sermon on "Keeping Children in School" exalts the profession of the schoolteacher to the plane which it really deserves. He says:

"I myself, if I could leave the preaching office and other things, or had to do so, would not be so glad to have any other work as that of the schoolmaster, or teacher of boys, for I know that this is the most useful, the greatest, and the best, next to the work of preaching. Indeed I scarcely know which of the two is better; for it is hard to make old dogs obedient and old rascals pious, and that is the work at which the preacher must labor, often in vain. But young trees can be better bent and trained, though some of them break in the process. Let it be one of the greatest virtues on earth faithfully to train other people's children; very few people, almost none in fact, do this for their own."

Christian fathers and mothers, however, can well be alarmed, and are in many cases, because their boys and girls are daily under the sculpturing influences of teachers who undermine the simple Christian faith of a little child. This also applies to professors in more advanced schools who tamper with the precious faith of young men, training for the ministry. What fearful judgments will fall upon the heads of such teachers! Christ's words, "It were better for him that a millstone be hung about his neck and he be cast into the depths of the sea, than that he should offend one of these little ones," have indeed been fulfilled in our day! With what agony has many a godly mother welcomed her son back from college, to find all her prayers and early teaching nullified, at least for the time being! It were better for nobody to be at the crossroads for youth, than for one in a position of trust to give false directions!—E. & L. Harvey.

AT THE CROSSROADS

> He stood at the crossroads all alone,
>   With the sunrise on his face;
> He had no fear for the path unknown,
>   He was set for a manly race.
> But the road stretched east, and the road stretched west;
> There was no one to tell him which way was the best.
>
> So my boy turned wrong and went down, down,
> Till he lost the race and the victor's crown,
> And fell at last in an ugly snare,
> Because no one stood at the crossroads there.

Another boy on another day
    At the selfsame crossroads stood;
He paused a moment to choose the way
    That would lead to the greater good.
And the road stretched east, and the road stretched west;
But I was there to show him the best.

So my boy turned right, and went on and on
Till he won the race and the victor's crown;
He came at last to the mansions fair,
Because I stood at the crossroads there.

Since then, I have raised a daily prayer
That I be kept standing faithfully there,
To warn the runners that go on by,
To save my own and another's boy.
                      —Selected.

    Many Sunday School superintendents and teachers plod on year after year with little thanks for their painstaking efforts. Could they but see the far-reaching results of their seemingly unnoticed work, they would take fresh heart.

THE HEART OF A CHILD

An angel paused in his onward flight,
With a seed of love, and truth, and right,
    And said, "Oh, where can this seed be sown,
    Where 'twill yield most fruit when fully grown?
To whom can this precious seed be given
That 'twill bear most fruit for earth and Heaven?"

The Savior heard and said as He smiled,
"Place it at once in the heart of a child."
    The angel whispered the blessed truth
    To a weary teacher of precious youth.
Her face grew brighter with heavenly light
As she led their thoughts in the ways of right.
                      —Anon.

THE TEACHER'S CROWN

Just a lump of clay in the potter's hands,
    Ugly and dirty and cold,
But the potter saw there a vessel so fair
    He with the clay would mold.
He worked with a will and cleansed it from dross;
He toiled with patience with not a moment's loss;
    He worked to a plan of beauty inwrought—
    And the vessel finished, by the king was bought,
Who would have thought that lump of clay
Would grace the courts of the king one day!

Just a boy or girl in your class today,
    With a heart so prone to sin,
But the Master sees there a soul so fair
    That through you He seeks to win.
So yield Him thy all—count not the cost;
Spend much time in prayer—that none be lost;
    Toil on in faith—that Christ they may own,
    For their place is with Him around the throne.
You would not think as they face you today,
Your crown of rejoicing they'll be for aye."

—Frank L. Tory.

God bless all the devoted sculptors of souls and grant many more Spirit-filled men and women to rise and help save our young generation from godlessness.

No matter what our station,
    No matter where we roam,
At times our thoughts will wander
    To our dear childhood's home,
Life's earliest recollections
    Of one's own kith and kin,
Those days by love surrounded,
    When mother tucked us in.

Oh, Mother, glorious Mother!
    Although we loved you so,
In those glad days of childhood,
    Your worth we did not know;
How many life successes,
    And honors we may win,
Are due to early memories,
    When mother tucked us in.
              —Clara Simpson.

CHAPTER XII

CHIPS FROM THE CHISEL

Mother is a physician when husband or child is sick.
  She is an interior decorator.
    She must be a good cook and dietician.
      She must be an expert on clothing repair.
        She must be a teacher and a child psychologist.
          She must often be a judge in settling arguments.
            She must be a purchasing agent, because she will manage at least 80% of the family income.
              She must be a bookkeeper to keep the budget and pay the bills.
                She must be a repairman who can replace a fuse, repair an electric cord, put oil on a squeaking hinge.
                  —*Review and Herald.*

MOTHER

It is a beautiful word—it, and its meaning;
It holds the feeling of warm arms in its sound,
And the comfort of a dear hand's soft caressing,
And through it old lost lullabies are found.

It is a tender word; it is the answer
To every helpless child's small desperate needs;
It is a holy word—a white fulfillment,
With something of Christ within its selfless deeds.

The simplicities of life are in its keeping;
The old sweet fragrance of milk and bread;
The scent of clean sheets through a dreamless sleeping;
The rustle of soft garments by a bed.

There is one word, my sister and my brother,
That God has written underneath His own;
One word—His intermediary—"Mother,"
Who shares the tasks He could not do alone.
                  —Grace Noll Crowell.

MOTHER'S BILL

A ten-year-old boy overheard a conversation about certain bills for services rendered which had to be paid, and conceived the idea of making out a bill for what work he had done. So the next morning he laid his statement of account on his mother's breakfast plate: "Mother owes Willie for carrying coal six times, 25 cents; for bringing water lots of times, 35 cents; for going ten errands, 30 cents; for being good twice, 10 cents; total: $1.00."

His mother read the bill but said nothing about it. That evening Willie found on his plate the dollar and also another bill, which read as follows: "Willie owes mother for his happy home for ten years, nothing; for his food and clothing, nothing; for nursing him in a long illness, nothing; for being good to him, nothing; total, nothing."

When Willie saw the dollar he was pleased, but when he read his mother's bill his eyes grew dim and his lips quivered. Then he took the money to his mother, threw his arms about her neck, and begged that she would let him do lots of things for her. Mother's bill is rarely presented, but it will pay each child to think it out and over for himself and then pay it—in loving obedience.—Selected.

TO MOTHER

It's wonderful, dear Mother, the many things you do,
You're such a very loving soul, we all rely on you;
And though you're sometimes sad,
You never let us know how much you sacrifice,
That's why we love you so.
—Selected.

TIED

She's tied at night, and in the day
She dare not be an hour away.

Tied by the feet and by the hands
In ways no mere man understands.

She has no time to think of looks;
She cannot read the latest books.

She cannot wander off alone;
Her eyes and ears are not her own.

Even her daily walks must be
Subject to whims of majesty.

Not long ago with lofty mien
She trod the earth—a reigning queen.

Now, she's a slave—with chains of gold—
To a young ruler three months old.
—Fay Inchfawn.

MOTHER

Our hearts hold you in loving thought,
    Dear Mother.
And is there one that place can fill?
    No other.
We thank you for your tender care,
Your goodness and your constant prayer,
    Dear Mother.

You were the first to coax and praise,
    Dear Mother.
You taught us how to love and serve
    Each other.
Your care we never can repay,
We're sure God blesses every day.
    Dear Mother.
—Clara Simpson.

"Where's mother?" is the question most frequently asked in many households. It is asked by the husband as well as the child coming in at nightfall: "Where's mother?" It is asked by the little ones when they get hurt and come in crying with the pain: "Where's mother?" It is asked by those who have seen some grand sight, heard some good news, or received some beautiful gift: "Where's mother?"

She sometimes feels wearied by the question, for they all ask it and keep asking it all the time. She is not only the first to hear every case of perplexity, but she is the judge in every court of domestic appeal. That is what puts the premature wrinkles on so many maternal foreheads and powders white so many maternal heads. You see it as a question that keeps on for all the years of childhood. It comes from the nursery and from the evening stand where the boys and girls are learning their school lesson, and from the starting out in the morning, when the tippet or hat or slate or book or overshoe is lost, until at night—all out of breath—the youngsters come in and shout until you can hear them from cellar to garret, and from front door to the back fence of the backyard: "Where's mother?"

Indeed, a child's life is so full of that question that, if he be taken away, one of the things that the mother most misses, and the silence that most oppresses her, is the absence of the question which she will never hear on earth again, except she hears it in a dream which sometimes restores the nursery just as it was, and then the voice comes back so natural, and so sweet, and so innocent, and so inquiring, that the dream breaks at the words, "Where's mother?"—Talmage.

WHERE'S MOTHER?

Bursting in from school or play,
This is what the children say,
Trooping, crowding, big and small,
On the threshold, in the hall,
Joining in the constant cry
Ever as the days go by—
   "Where's Mother?"

From the weary bed of pain,
This same question comes again;
From the boy with sparkling eyes,
Bearing home his earliest prize;
From the bronzed and bearded son—
   "Where's Mother?"

Burdened with our lonely task,
One day we may vainly ask
For the rest of her embrace.
Let us love her while we may;
Well for us that we can say—
   "Where's Mother?"

Mother, with untiring hands,
At the post of duty stands,
Patient, seeking not her own,
Anxious for the good alone
Of the children as they cry,
Ever as the days go by—
 "Where's Mother?"
—Selected.

MOTHER'S REST

The porridge is lumpy, the butter is short,
 Cold is the tea and stale the bread,
Nothing and nobody's quite as they ought—
 Mother is taking a day in bed.

Jimmy has fallen and cut both knees,
 Father was late in getting away,
The grocer's boy has forgotten the cheese—
 Mother is having a peaceful day.

A steamroller's working outside the door,
 The Daily Lady's feeling depressed;
She "don't believe she can't come no more"—
 Mother is having a lovely rest.

Teatime comes and the fire is bright,
 A feeling of comfort is in the air;
Everyone's comfortable, everything's right—
 Mother has given it up in despair.
—Molly Capes.

MEMORIES!

As you think of your own mother, remembering
 her with love and gratitude—
  in wistful yearning
   or lonely longing . . .
 I am quite sure that the memories that warm and
 soften your heart are not at all like the memories
 the children of today will have . . .
For you are, no doubt, remembering the smell of the
 starch in your mother's apron,
  or the smell of a newly ironed blouse,
   the smell of newly baked bread,
    the fragrance of the violets she had pinned on her breast.

It would be such a pity if all that one could remember would be the aroma of toasted tobacco or nicotine and the offensive odor of beer on the breath!
—Peter Marshall.

(From his book of sermons, *Mr. Jones, Meet the Master*, Peter Davies, Ltd.)

TO MY MOTHER

I love you Mother for your quiet grace,
For that dear smile upon your kindly face,
For marks of toil upon each loving hand,
That worked for me ere I could understand;
For all time's touches on your hair and brow,
For never were you quite so dear as now.
I will be loyal, faithful, loving, true,
For, Mother dear, I owe so much to you.
—Clara Simpson.

DEAR MOTHER O' MINE

Little things mean so much to Mother—
  A quick caress or a sunny smile,
Willing hands that give loving service—
  All help to make her toil worthwhile.

Little things mean so much to Mother—
  A bitter word or an angry frown
Hushes the song on her lips to silence
  While on her day the sun goes down.

Little things mean so much to Mother—
  Which shall it be, dear Mother o' mine?
Words that fill all your days with shadows,
  Or smiles that carry their own sunshine?
—Selected.

MOTHER MINE

O Mother mine, when I was small,
You seemed to me my all in all;
The sunshine shimmered in your face;
The flowers blossomed in your grace.

You laughed with me when I was gay
And kissed my childish tears away—
Mother dearie, Mother cheery, Mother mine.

O Mother, as the years rolled o'er
Our heads, I loved you more and more.
When weakness laid its hand on you,
You were so patient, brave, and true;
You seemed the sum of all things good;
My dream of perfect womanhood—
Mother dearie, Mother cheery, Mother mine.

O Mother mine, if I can be
To little ones who look to me,
A mother half as sweet and wise
And tender; if they but surmise
That in your likeness I have tried
To grow, I shall be satisfied—
Mother dearie, Mother cheery, Mother mine.
—Selected.

MY MOTHER...

When the Master Artist made her,
    All that was good or grand,
All that was fair and lovely
    He brought to the task in hand.

He walked among the flowers
    In the garden of the skies,
Mated two jewels of luster;
    And gave her stars for eyes.

He caught the white sea spindrift
    In the shining, sunlit air,
Wove it in strands of silver
    And made my mother's hair.

He sent a soft breeze straying
    Where song birds sing from choice
And when it had caught the cadence
    My mother had her voice.

Then out from the glowing gateway
    Where the sun's last plunders pile,
He beckoned a glimmer of glory
    And shaped her warm, sweet smile.

And last He gathered the roses
    That grew o'er a low stone wall,
Crushed all their crimson petals,
    Crushed them, and let them fall.

And up from the ground, rose fragrant,
    As up from a censer-bowl,
The incense with which He fashioned
    The breath of my mother's soul.
        —Nell Ruth Roff.

BEAUTIFUL MOTHER

The peachbloom's gone from off her cheek,
    The gloss has left her hair,
Her wrinkled hands are thin and weak,
    Her brow is seamed with care;
But oh, of all the loveliness
    That robes the soul with grace,
I have not seen such beauty-dress
    As mother's winsome face!

The love-light shining in her eyes,
    The peace that in them sleeps,
The tender smile that e'er a while
    Brings sunshine to her lips,
The saintly lines of character,
    All chiseled by God's hand—
Ah! life has wrought its best in her,
    And angels understand.

So beautiful she seems to me;
    Of all sweet things refined,
Her body a transparency
    Through which her soul hath shined.
Say not 'tis faded beauty, hers,
    For what is beauty's prime?
'Tis growing old with Heaven's gold
    To crown its harvest time.
        —Selected.

MY MOTHER...

Someone I love comes back to me
With every gentle face I see;
Beneath each wave of soft, grey hair
I seem to see my mother there.
With every kindly grace and word
It seems as if I must have heard
Her speak, and felt her tender gaze
With all the love of olden days,
And I am moved to take her hand
And tell her now I understand
How tired she grew beneath the strain
Of feeling every loved one's pain.

No further burdens could she bear;
The promise of that land so fair
Alone could tempt her from her child;
And now, if I could keep her here,
No sacrifice would be too dear,
No tempered winds for her too mild.
Then I would smooth and kiss her face,
And by her side take my old place,
And sob my fears and cares away,
The tears I have so long repressed
Would lose their ache upon her breast.
I think if I could feel her touch
Once more, it would not matter much
How sunny or how dark the day.
—Unknown.

TIRED HANDS

Folded they lie upon her tranquil breast,
My Mother's tired hands, their labor done,
Knotted and scarred in battles they have won,
Worn to the quick by love's unkind behest;
Pulseless they lie, while from the crimson west
A flood of her glory from the setting sun
Shines on her face; I hear the deep "Well done,"
God's angelus that calls her soul to rest.
Found is the Holy Grail of knightly quest,
Here in her home where such brave deeds were done
As knight ne'er saw since chivalry begun.
She suffered, toiled, and died; God knows the rest,
And if Christ's crown shines not above her cross
Then all is loss, immeasurable loss.
—Clarence Hawks.

GOD BLESS MOTHER

O beautiful for little feet,
    You've guided on the way
To manhood and to womanhood,
    No one can thee repay!
O mother, dear, O mother, dear,
    God shed His love on thee,
And may thy children love to serve,
    To conquer and be free.
                  —Selected.

TRUE LOVELINESS

My mother's face is wrinkled now,
And not so soft and fair,
And silvery threads are shining where
Once there was jet black hair;
But when I see the love light shine
From out her dimming eyes,
It seems but a reflection from
The gates of paradise.

Her hands, once soft and lovely,
Are thin and aged now;
But oh, how many, many times
They've soothed some aching brow.
They might not seem so lovely if
Their shape alone you see,
But oh, I know their deeds of love—
They're beautiful to me.

Her steps are feeble, faltering,
That once were firm and light.
How many steps her feet have made
By day as well as night!
She may seem old to others—not
So beautiful to see;
But she'll always be the loveliest
Of all on earth to me.
                  —Anon.

REGRETS

I wish I had said more. So long, so long
    About your simple tasks I watched you, dear
    I knew you craved the words you did not hear;
I knew your spirit, brave and chaste and strong,
Was wistful that it might not do the wrong;
    And all its wistfulness and all its fear
    Were in your eyes whenever I was near,
And yet you always went your way with song.
Oh, prodigal of smiles for other eyes,
    I led my life. At last there came a day
    When with some careless praise I turned away
From what you fashioned for a sweet surprise.
And now it is too late for me to pour
My vase of myrrh. Would God I had said more !
                        —Selected.

MOTHER'S SACRIFICE

She gave the best of her life, with joy, for me;
She robbed herself with loving heart, unstintingly.
For me, with willing hands she toiled from day to day;
For me, she prayed, when headstrong youth would have its way.
Her loving arms, my cradle once, are weary now;
And time has set the seal of care upon her brow,
And though no other eyes than mine their meaning trace,
I read my history in the lines of her dear face.
'Mongst gems of Him Who showers gifts on shining sands,
I count her days as pearls that fall from His kind hands.
                        —Selected.

WANTED

A woman who can see things;
  Who can feel needs;
    Who can be stirred deeply by lacks;
      Who will refuse to be complacent when chaos reigns;
        Who suffers when good causes suffer;
          Who believes with all her might that bad things
            And dead organizations
              And lame methods

And indifferent people
  And languishing enterprises
    And untouched opportunities need
      not remain such;
        Who never despairs over any situation;
          Who hopes a way, who sees a way out—
            or is out seeking the way;
              Who dares to say, "I know,"
                on the basis of her faith;
                  Who is always sure,
                    though never dead sure;
                      Who spreads a contagion of
                        hopefulness wherever she goes.

A woman who having seen a worthy end, works toward it—
  Though it be ten thousand miles away;
    Who believes that anything worth believing in is worth working for;
      Who produces forces, and marshals forces where
        they are not at hand;
          Who, charged with energy, charges others;
            Who puts ginger into all that she does and
              leaves out the mustard and the vinegar;
                Who is humble enough to accept "nobody's
                  business" as her business;
                    Who says, "Come on, let's do it"—
                      and then does it whether anybody else
                        comes on or not."—*Gleanings.*

MOTHERS THE WORLD NEEDS

Mothers with courage; mothers who pray,
These are the kind the world needs today.
  Mothers who think, who study and plan;
  Mothers who laugh as much as they can,
Having the gift that is better than money —
The habit of seeing that some things are funny.
  Mothers whose faith never wavers or falters;
  Mothers whose spirits the world never alters;
Loving the right and scorning the wrong;
Facing the problems of life with a song.

Mothers whose bravery transcends their fears;
  Winning the battle with patience and tears;
Never submitting to weakness or sin—
Storming Heaven's gates till the children are in.
  Mothers heroic, not guilty of whining;
  Hands graced with service and faces with shining.
Mothers of purity, virtue, and faith,
Steadfast in life and triumphant in death;
  Looking beyond the dark pathway of sorrow,
  Seeking a home in God's joyous tomorrow,
Leading the children; pointing the way—
These are the mothers the world needs today!
            —Kathryn Blackburn Peck.

MOTHER'S QUESTION

I think ofttimes as the night draws nigh
    Of an old house on the hill,
Of a yard all wide and blossomed-starred
    Where the children played at will.
And when the night at last came down,
    Hushing the merry din,
Mother would look around and ask,
    "Are all the children in?"

'Tis many and many a year since then,
    And the old house on the hill
No longer echoes to childish feet,
    And the yard is still, so still.
But I see it all, as the shadows creep,
    And though many the years have been
Since then, I can still hear Mother ask,
    "Are all the children in?"

I wonder, if when the shadows fall
    On the last short, earthly day,
When we say good-bye to the world outside,
    All tired with our childish play,
And we step out into that Other Land
    Where Mother so long has been,
We will hear her ask, as of olden times,
    "Are all the children in?"
                —Selected.

PRAYER FOR THE CHILDREN

Father, our children keep!
We know not what is coming on the earth;
Beneath the shadow of Thy heavenly wing,
O keep them, keep them, Thou Who gav'st them birth.

Father, draw nearer us!
Draw firmer round us Thy protecting arm;
Oh, clasp our children closer to Thy side,
Uninjured in the day of earth's alarm.

Them, in Thy chambers hide!
Oh, hide them and preserve them calm and safe,
When sin abounds and error flows abroad,
And Satan tempts, and human passions chafe.

O keep them undefiled!
Unspotted from a tempting world of sin;
That, clothed in white, through the bright city gates,
They may with us in triumph enter in.
—Horatius Bonar.

TO MY SON!

Do you know that your soul is of my soul such part,
That you seem to be fiber and core of my heart?
None other can pain me as you, dear, can do;
None other can please me or praise as you.

Remember, the world will be quick with its blame,
If shadow or shame ever darken your name;
"Like mother, like son," is a saying so true,
The world will judge largely of mother by you.

Be this, then, your task—if task it shall be,
To force this proud world to do homage to me;
Be sure it will say when its verdict you've won,
"She reaps as she sowed, Lo! this man is her son."
—Your Mother.

A PRAYER FOR A SON

As Thou didst walk the lanes of Galilee,
So, loving Savior, walk with him for me;
For since the years have passed, and he is grown,
I cannot follow: he must walk alone.

Be Thou my feet that I have had to stay,
For Thou canst comrade him on every way;
Be Thou my voice when sinful things allure,
Pleading with him to choose those that endure;
Be Thou my hand that would keep his in mine,
And all things else that Mother must resign.

When he was little, I could walk and guide;
But now, I pray that Thou be at his side.
And, as Thy blessed Mother guided Thee,
So, loving Savior, guard my son for me.
—Unknown.

THE WATCHER

She always leaned to watch for us,
    Anxious if we were late,
In winter by the window,
    In summer by the gate.

And though we mocked her tenderly
    Who had such foolish care,
The long way home would seem more safe
    Because she waited there.

Her thoughts were all so full of us—
    She never could forget!
And so I think that where she is
    She must be watching yet.

Waiting till we come home to her,
    Anxious if we are late—
Watching from Heaven's window,
    Leaning from Heaven's gate.
—Margaret Widdermer.

Most of us have a mother watching and waiting for news of our victory or defeat. If she be not sitting at a window of earth, she is sitting at a window of Heaven, and she is going to hear all about it; not according to our talents or educational equipment or our opportunity, but according as to whether God is for us or against us.

—Talmage.

Books for Children and Young People

Asking Father *by E. F. & L. Harvey & Trudy Harvey Tait*
A series of short, factual stories showing the wonderful interest and concern of our Heavenly Father as He delights to answer the prayers of His people. Parents enjoy reading this book as much as their children. It is also an excellent source of material for young people's meetings.

Father Calling *by E. F. & L. Harvey & Trudy Harvey Tait*
This companion to Asking Father relates the childhood experiences of such famous Christians as C. H. Spurgeon, Adam Clarke, Samuel Chadwick, Ida Scudder, and others, showing how God spoke to them at an early age, thus preparing them for their unique place in His divine plan.

Jessica's First Prayer *by Hesba Stretton*
To Jessica, a poor outcast girl on the streets of London who has to beg or steal to keep herself alive, Mr. Daniel's coffee stall becomes, for a few moments each week, a little paradise. The unlikely pair are influenced by each other in striking ways: Jessica comes to a knowledge of the God Who answers prayer, and Mr. Daniel is brought to repentance for his life of meanness and covetousness.

Eric, Or Little by Little *by F. W. Farrar*
An extremely poignant story of a popular schoolboy's descent into evil at an English boarding school. The author shows graphically that the descent into sin is most often akin to a slow leak rather than a blowout. This book has been the means of numerous conversions.

The Christian's Daily Challenge

by Edwin and Lillian Harvey

This daily devotional is a treasury of spiritual wisdom for preachers and writers and an excellent gift for ministers, missionaries, and Christian workers. It is a feast of fat things for the growing Christian and a stimulus to all of us to run faithfully the race which is set before us.

- Each reading begins with Scripture.

- Almost 250 authors are quoted.

- Emphasis on Bible reading and prayer.

- Complete index of authors, and

- Complete index of Scripture texts.

Sample titles include: "God Polishes His Own," "Shut in With God," "The Godly Shall Suffer," "Salvation from Worry," and "Life Blood for Lasting Results."

"Then he said unto them, go your way, eat the fat, and drink the sweet, and send portions to them for whom nothing is prepared" (Neh. 8:10).